LIVING WITH MURDER

FAMILIES LEFT BEHIND

YVONNE KINSELLA

Gill & Macmillan

Gill & Macmillan Ltd
Hume Avenue, Park West, Dublin 12
with associated companies throughout the world
www.gillmacmillan.ie

© Yvonne Kinsella 2009
978 07171 4589 8

Type design: Make Communication
Print origination by Carole Lynch
Printed in the UK by CPI Mackays, Chatham ME5 8TD

This book is typeset in Linotype Minion and Neue
Helvetica.

5 4 3 2 1

This book is dedicated to all the families featured, who, every day of the week, are living with murder.

ACKNOWLEDGMENTS

Firstly, and most sincerely, I wish to thank the families and friends of all of the innocent victims whose stories I have featured in this book and in the documentary *Living with Murder* on TV3. Their courage and strength is beyond belief and I am extremely grateful to them for allowing me into their lives. I hope their stories will touch the hearts of everyone who picks up this book and give readers some idea of the heartache and pain endured on a daily basis by anyone who has lost a family member in such a horrific and devastating way.

Thanks to Gill & Macmillan for giving me the opportunity to write these stories and to Sarah Liddy for her invaluable help in editing them. To Sideline Productions, Billie and Ruth, for trusting me. To Yvonne Nolan, the series producer of the programme and a good friend, for asking me to produce the programme in the first place and for always being there at the end of the phone day and night. To Eoin Kavanagh, Catherine Quinn and Conor Connolly who were a great production team, great pals and great support from start to finish. To retired Detective Inspector Brian Sherry, I can't find enough words to thank you, Brian, for all your help, you really are a star! Thanks to John Kerins and Niall Moonan in the *Irish Mirror*, Barry Cummins in RTÉ, one particular high-ranking garda in Dublin South and one in Dublin North—you both know who you are. Thanks to journalist Mick McCaffrey for digging things up for me when I needed them and to journalist Conor Lally and all of the contributors who took part in the programme.

To my mam Sylvia, sister Jackie, brother-in-law Ed and mother-in-law Stella for all your help and support over the past few months in so many ways.

And last, but not least, to my husband John and my children Darren and Shannon—it's only when you meet families such as those I have spoken to whilst writing this book, that you realise just how precious your children are and how every moment with them is priceless.

Yvonne Kinsella
April 2009

CONTENTS

INTRODUCTION

Three decades ago, in a very different Ireland, people would have reacted with shock to news reports of a man murdering his wife, a woman her husband, a father his child or to news of an innocent bystander losing his or her life simply because they were 'in the wrong place at the wrong time'.

Unfortunately, for all of us, things are very different today and hearing news of a fatal shooting, a vicious stabbing or a brutal beating has become almost a weekly—and sometimes daily—occurrence. Also unfortunately, murder is now so commonplace that we barely take any notice. In fact, when it comes to the 'wiping out' of a criminal some of us simply shrug our shoulders and say, 'That's one less thug on our streets.'

In 1960, there were three murders in Ireland; by 2007 that figure had shot up to a worrying 78. It's a frightening statistic for such a small country with a population of only 4.5 million. Because of the selfish action of others, many innocent families have been left with only memories, old photographs or video footage of people they held so close to their hearts.

Today, it seems, life is cheap. As criminal gangs battle to take control of the streets and the huge drug empires that line them, a life can be taken for as little as €100—the cost to hire a gun on some street corners in Dublin and Limerick. And if some innocent person is caught in the crossfire as one crime lord attacks another, well, putting it simply and in their terms, that's life! These narrow-minded, uneducated gang members have no feelings when it comes to cashing in on the demand for drugs on our streets—and they will stop at nothing to get what they want.

But, unfortunately, it's not just gang bosses who are causing the murder rate to rise at such a rapid rate. Over the past few months, I have been privileged to be allowed in to the lives of many families affected by many different types of murder.

I've spoken to people left heartbroken by unprovoked, callous attacks on members of their family in the form of strangulation, shootings, arson or vicious beatings. All of these victims were people living an honest life and doing their best, not knowing the evil that lay around the corner. Some of the families have been affected by crimes of passion, where a boyfriend strangles his lover in an act of jealousy, or a husband smothers his wife for reasons known only to himself.

I have also seen the devastation left behind by what we label 'familicide'—a sickening, albeit descriptive, term used when someone, for whatever personal reason, decides to take the lives of the other members of their family—one or more children and their spouse—before finally killing themselves. This is probably the most horrific and upsetting form of murder today, as it can mean three or four lives are taken in an instant.

While striving to understand what has caused Ireland to become such a murderous state, I have interviewed many people to find out what life is like for those left behind. As they struggle to pick up the pieces, they talk about how they are constantly battling to come to terms with the sudden and brutal killing of their loved ones.

They have let me inside their homes and their hearts as they remember the day their son, daughter, brother, sister or partner was brutally murdered. And they tell us how the young children of the victims are coping with the loss of their mammy or daddy.

There are families still waiting for someone to be charged with the murder of their loved ones. The members of these families talk about the anguish and torment of not being able to get justice for the person who has been killed. Others tell us their personal views, derived from their own experiences, of the Irish criminal justice system. Of what they think of the punishment these killers have received from the courts and of the possibility of bringing back the death penalty in Ireland.

All reveal what they really think of the evil men who destroyed their lives.

This book is a testament to these Irish people who, through no fault of their own, are now *Living With Murder.*

Yvonne Kinsella
March 2009

01 | CAUGHT IN THE CROSSFIRE

ANTHONY CAMPBELL

On 12 December 2006, just two weeks before Christmas, 20-year-old Anthony Campbell left his dad's flat in St Michan's House in Dublin's north inner city to earn a bit of extra cash for the holidays. He was happy to have been offered a day's work with a plumber, fixing radiators at a house in Finglas on the outskirts of the city.

Anthony had returned to Ireland three years earlier, having spent most of his life in London, but he had stayed in contact with his dad throughout his time in England. Despite his Cockney accent, he had fitted in almost immediately with the lads in his dad's flats complex. He had started playing soccer and had helped set up a soccer team with his new mates. He had got a position as an apprentice plumber, but, unfortunately, like a lot of people in trades at the time in Ireland, work had become scarce and he had been let go a few weeks earlier. He had been worried about being able to afford presents for his family for Christmas, and having some money to spend with his friends over the holidays, so the offer of a bit of work came at exactly the right time. He had had some reservations about returning to Ireland but, despite his work problems, coming back home had worked out for him. Things were going well.

Anthony was very well liked by everyone who knew him and was his usual happy-go-lucky self as he headed off that morning in his new employer's van.

When Anthony and his boss arrived at the house in Scribblestown, they got out of the van and headed to the house.

What they didn't know was that, only yards away, two assailants were lying in wait ready to carry out a hit on crime lord Martin 'Marlo' Hyland, who was sleeping in an upstairs room of the house, which, in fact, belonged to his niece.

Before Hyland's niece left the house to drop her child to school, she told Anthony and his boss that someone was asleep upstairs, and that they were not to go near that bedroom. Anthony's employer told Anthony to start work bleeding the downstairs radiators while he headed off to get some supplies. When he returned a short time later, he couldn't get into the house. He rang the doorbell repeatedly, banged on the door and rang Anthony's mobile several times. When there was no answer, he started to panic.

As Anthony's boss was trying to see into the house, one of Hyland's henchmen arrived to deliver the morning newspaper to his pal. At the same time, Hyland's niece arrived home and she was the one who opened the door. No one was prepared for the bloody scene that greeted them. Lying on his back on the floor was young Anthony. Initially, they thought he had collapsed, as they didn't notice any blood, but they soon realised that this innocent young man had been shot and left to die beside the radiator he was fixing at the front window of the house.

Conor Lally, crime reporter with *The Irish Times* remembers the day only too well.

He was in a taxi driving along the quays, heading into work, when he got a phone call from a garda contact telling him that Marlo Hyland had been shot dead. The officer also told him that a young man who was working in the house at the time had also been killed. Lally's plans for the day had to be put on hold as the double murder took precedence over everything.

He immediately headed to Scribblestown, to the house where the attack had taken place. By the time he arrived, the media scrum had already begun and camera crews, journalists and photographers were gathered waiting for more information on what had happened that morning. Conor knew that this was going to be a really big story.

Hyland had been very heavily involved in gangland crime, armed robbery and drug dealing for just over a decade. By the time he was killed, he was running the biggest drugs empire in the country. He and his gang specialised in sourcing large quantities of wholesale cocaine, heroin and other potentially lethal drugs. He also helped junior criminals to plan armed raids. Hyland was the man to talk to if you needed to source a car or a gun to carry out a gangland hit or a robbery. He could supply anything that was needed for any crime.

'He was involved in every aspect of organised crime that you could think of,' says Lally. 'In the year and a half before he was killed, anytime senior gardaí gave a security briefing to the likes of Bertie Ahern, there was one name that cropped up all the time, it was Hyland. He was the most active gangland leader around at the time of his death.'

In complete contrast, Anthony Campbell had simply gone to work that morning to earn some money for Christmas.

———

What is known is that someone came to the front door of the house and, as Anthony answered the door, two gunmen walked in. The gardaí believe that one of the gunmen held Anthony downstairs whilst the other went upstairs and shot Hyland several times as he slept. The gunman then came back downstairs and shot Anthony Campbell in the head. Anthony had tried to save himself by shielding his head with his hands as the gunman fired a .45 semi-automatic handgun at his face. The fatal bullet passed through his left hand before entering his head.

Anthony was killed for one reason and one reason only—because he answered the door to the wrong people. The men who shot Hyland knew the criminal well and had expected him to answer the door. They didn't wear balaclavas, in fact, they didn't wear any disguises at all. When somebody they weren't expecting opened the door, they knew that they would have to kill him because he would be able to identify them to the guards. Anthony Campbell was coldly executed to keep the two killers out of jail.

In the year before Hyland was killed, gardaí had set up a target operation called Operation Oak—and Hyland was its main objective. Operation Oak was dedicated to keeping Hyland and his crew under surveillance and it led to more than 20 members of Hyland's gang being caught with drugs, firearms and large sums of money. In the months prior to the hit, Hyland had become more involved than ever in criminal activity and was dabbling in anything that would make large amounts of easy cash.

But Hyland's prowess was only one side of the story. To his cronies and rival gangs, he was getting too big for his boots. The attention the gardaí were showing to Hyland had a knock-on effect on those in his own circle. If Hyland was being watched, then so were they, and this caused a lot of tension. Small-time gang members were being stopped and searched day in, day out often as they drove around their own areas. And during these searches, the guards were regularly finding stashes of guns and drugs. These gang members blamed Hyland for the fact that many were facing jail terms of up to 10 years—and all because Hyland was drawing attention to himself.

There seemed only one way to stop it all and that was to take Hyland out of the equation. Gardaí believe that members of Hyland's gang planned his execution meticulously—and Anthony Campbell just happened to be at the house when the hit took place.

In the hours after Hyland was shot, there was a lot of speculation that Anthony was somehow involved in organised crime. It was reasoned that he must have known Hyland, but any confusion was cleared up quickly. By noon that day, we all knew that Anthony Campbell was just working in the house, that he was an innocent victim and that he was killed because he would have been able to identify the people who had killed Hyland.

When Christine Campbell had woken on the morning of 12 December 2006, she had expected to spend the day doing some Christmas shopping in town. She had the day off work and still had some last-minute bits and pieces to pick up before the Christmas rush. She had planned to get her son, Anthony, her only child, a shirt and she wanted to buy some more presents for her parents. She was looking forward to her trip into the city centre. She never expected that day to be the worst of her life.

'On the morning it happened, I wasn't meant to be in work but my supervisor rang and asked me to do her a favour,' Christine says. 'As I was coming off my break at a quarter to eleven, I got a phone call from Anthony's dad's partner, she was frantic on the other end of the line. She was so hysterical that she just blurted out, "It's Anthony, he's been shot dead." In fairness to Edel, she had just been told and she was just in shock, it was just pure this-is-not-happening kind of thing. When she said it to me, I just stood there in shock with the phone in my hand and I said, "He can't be", and I just cut her off. I just remember feeling this cold rush all over my body, as if my body had switched off. I asked a lady that works with me if she had heard anything on the news about a shooting. I think she knew something was up because I must have turned a funny colour. I could just feel everything draining out of me. She said, "There's after being something on the radio; two men shot in Finglas." Then she said, "What's up with you?" and I told her, "I'm after getting a phone call saying me son is after being shot. But my son is gone to work." That was my reaction.'

Christine left work immediately and went over to the flat Anthony shared with his father. She was met with a chaotic scene where no one knew what had happened. Christine kept expecting Anthony to walk through the door, hoping that he would suddenly appear and be embarrassed at all the fuss. But that never happened.

The days that followed were a blur to Christine and Anthony's whole family. They were in a daze, with hundreds of unanswered questions racing through their minds. Although people sympathised with them and offered support, the reality of what had happened was just too much for Christine to take in.

'We were all in bits. None of us could understand what had happened. How Anthony had been killed. Why? We were all just in shock,' she says. 'The guards couldn't tell us much, just that Anthony was killed and the other fella was killed, but other than that, we didn't know what was going on. We were taken out to this place in Marino to identify Anthony's body. It was just like a shed, a horrible place. They were very formal with us and they told us "not to touch the body", obviously for forensics, which is totally understandable, but how can you tell a mother not to touch her dead child? It's what every mother wants to do in that situation, hold on to her child. Let him know that you're there. When we finally got in to see him, he was lying there on a slab. He had a sheet over him and it was then, when I looked at him lying there, that I finally realised it was true. It was actually him. My Anthony. I just kept thinking there's my child, lying there dead. I wasn't allowed go near him, and I found that very, very hard and I'll never forget it. I thought they should have let me just touch him. I was standing there looking at my baby, and all I wanted to do was to hold him.'

Christine's world was turned upside down. The faint hope she had clung on to that there had been some terrible mistake, that it wasn't Anthony who had been shot, disappeared in the split second she saw her son's lifeless body. It was her worst nightmare.

There was a turmoil of emotions running through her, which she only recognised later. 'I've never known emotions like it and I wouldn't wish it on anyone. It took me five days to actually kiss my son. Five days to build up the courage to kiss my own flesh and blood. I suppose I knew that once I kissed him and felt his skin, there was no going back. And when I did, he felt like velvet. He was so soft.'

Over and over again, Christine kept asking herself, Why me? Why Anthony? Violence, drugs and guns were not a part of their lives and she had never expected that her son would become another statistic in the drug gangs' feuding.

Christine had never been worried about Anthony. He wasn't overly streetwise but as he never got into any trouble, she didn't see this as a problem. She told him the same thing that all mothers tell their children, 'Don't get into trouble. Be careful.' His safety was always in the back of her mind, but she knew she didn't have to worry too much and he never caused her any problems. She was secretly pleased that he sometimes had trouble getting into clubs because he looked so young—even though it upset him a bit—but he never let that sort of thing ruin his night. 'He was a great kid,' she says, 'a great son.'

This is why she finds it so hard to accept that Anthony died the way he did. 'If he had died through cancer or some other illness, I'd have been able to nurse him, sit with him and have some time with him,' Christine says. 'I'd have been able to do what you normally do, what everyone else does when someone is dying of a sickness, but the fact that he was taken away from us in such a horrific way kills me. Because as normal as our lives were up to that day, nothing will ever be the same again, it's changed forever.'

To everyone who knew him, Anthony was a warm-hearted man and he had an impact on everyone he met. His friends have all talked about his good humour, how he loved nothing more than a game of soccer, a few pints in the local and a game of pool—though he didn't like losing and was very competitive. He was a regular 20-year-old who liked socialising with his friends and was always up for the craic. The impact of his death was far wider than just his family and his friends, who still visit his grave and place flowers in memory of their beloved pal.

'All I have now is a grave,' says Christine. 'And I go at least once a week, sometimes two or three times. It depends on the weather really, but I never miss it. I just busy myself doing little things. Just to stay for a while. I'll take the flowers out of the pots and then I'll wash the headstone down, just fix it all up and clean it. I'll just sit there and I'll read the verse that's on the headstone and it makes me think. He's in my thoughts 24/7.'

Since Anthony's death, Christine has thrown herself into her work. She doesn't like taking days off and likes to keep busy all the time. 'I have a mixture of emotions, some mornings are good and some mornings are dreadful. Some mornings I don't want to get out of bed but I know I have to. If I get a bad morning there's nothing I can do. My life was fine up until 12 December 2006. I know everyone has their struggles, everyone has to go to work, that has never bothered me. I always had something to live for and I lived for Anthony. I used to say to him joking, "Don't make me a grandmother early", stuff like that. Now I'm sorry I ever said that. It's the little things like that I regret.'

For Christine, it is as if someone has taken away her soul and she struggles to accept that she has to live her life without her child, the one person she lived for. 'The one person that made me tick in this life is gone. I don't think I'll ever be the same again. Nothing will ever make me tick the way Anthony did. He was my only child. He was all I had and now I don't think anything will ever be the same again. We could talk to one another about anything. And we always had a laugh. There was no awkwardness between us and for instance, if I went over to him, even in front of his friends, he'd have no problem giving me a kiss on the cheek. He wasn't shy about showing his affection or vice versa. We were very close.'

People suggested that she should talk to someone outside of the family, a professional, who may help her to come to terms with what had happened. Although she was initially reluctant, Christine finally realised that bottling up her feelings was not doing her any good and that to move on, she needed help.

'I have a counsellor now, Dennis, who comes to me every week and I have to say he's been brilliant,' she says. 'It's good to be able to talk to someone who is not part of all this. I know I'll never get closure, I'll never be the same again, but what I'm actually trying to get is acceptance and justice. They are the two goals that I've got.'

Christine has stopped aiming for things in her own life, she pours all her energy into getting justice for Anthony—the last thing she can do for him. It is tough at times and, 18 months after his murder, she is no closer to knowing who killed her son. But she can't let go and knows she has to keep pushing for justice. Her one hope is that someone will be tried and convicted for Anthony's murder. She believes that she would get some peace of mind if she knew that someone was in prison.

Christine says she tries not to think of the man who pulled the trigger. She doesn't think it was something a normal person could do. The killer thought nothing about taking her child's life that morning, thought nothing of the impact on Anthony's family, on his friends and of the devastation it would cause. 'If these people had any morals,' she says, 'they wouldn't be able to sleep at night. My son wasn't even a man, he was a child of 20 years of age, and he was just killed.'

The hardest thing for Christine is to think about is how Anthony must have felt on that morning. It is something that is never far from her mind. She wonders what he would have been thinking and feeling as he heard the gunshot upstairs—or if he didn't hear anything. She still doesn't have the full picture and the gardaí don't tell her much. She thinks that the gardaí are probably trying to protect her, but she wants to know the truth. She wants to know what actually happened that morning. Because no one has been caught yet, there is still a great deal of red tape surrounding the case and the guards are only obliged to tell her so much. It's something Christine finds distressing. She understands that they are doing their job, doing as much as they can, but, for Christine, the not knowing is worse than the grieving. 'If I knew what happened, instead of all the time playing out different scenarios in my mind, maybe I could be at peace with myself. I think I deserve to know the truth. But I don't think I'll hear the real story until those responsible are charged and brought to court. Over and over again I ask myself, How could someone do this? How could a man pull a trigger on an innocent defenceless kid? What kind of person does that? Does he ever think about the devastation he's left behind? My family will never be the same again without Anthony.'

People ask Christine if she is bitter. But she can't explain her emotions in those terms—she is heartbroken. She is dealing with what has happened the best she can but after the death of a child—especially in such horrific circumstances—she feels she has lost everything. 'You bury your future,' she says. 'That's the only way I can put it. That's how I feel about it. There is no future for me now.'

A few months after Anthony's death, Christine visited a medium to see if she could connect with him. The medium told her that Anthony is around her all the time and that he was the one giving her strength and support, urging her on. It's something that Christine takes comfort from. She does feel her son is still with her—as odd as she knows it may sound—and that he is pushing her in the right direction.

Christine has so many good memories of her only child. She feels blessed that she was his mother and thankful for the time that she had with him.

———

Christine and Anthony moved to London when he was 14 months old. Christine's parents, Carmel and Louis, helped to rear him whilst Christine worked to make ends meet. 'He was a great kid,' Carmel says. 'One day his teacher told him that Louis wasn't his "biological Dad". He said, "I don't care, he's my dad and that's that." It was quite funny really, because his granddad was always his dad, but I was always his nanny.'

Anthony was a typical little boy, always up to devilment, though he was clever too. He loved the trips around London that his granddad would take him on and he loved history. When they were out together, Anthony was always asking questions. Carmel remembers that Anthony wouldn't rest until he knew everything.

At first, Christine and Anthony lived with Carmel and Louis but eventually they got their own place. They still saw each other all the time, though, and theirs was a loving, close-knit family. Christine was used to having Anthony near her, it was the way things were done in London, where children were brought everywhere with you. 'In Ireland people would have got babysitters but even the pubs cater for kids in London, so anywhere I went, Anthony went.'

Louis and Carmel moved back to Dublin when Anthony was ten years old, and Christine and Anthony stayed in London for another seven or eight years.

Carmel and Louis still can't come to terms with Anthony's death. When they talk of him, they cry. Especially his grandfather, who suffered a stroke shortly after Anthony was killed—he just cannot bring himself to reminisce about the little boy who called him Daddy.

'We miss him so much,' Carmel says. 'Those men have no idea how much devastation they caused the day they took Anthony away from us. It's very hard to cope. We see him every day. He looks down on us, with all his other cousins, in photos all around the house. So it's very hard not to think about him. He was such a big part of our lives. When we heard the news that day, we were just sick. We forgot that he was working in Finglas and we kept thinking it couldn't be him. But when it hits you, it's just a nightmare. We all have a cry every now and then. It's hard not to. That first Christmas was horrible and then we had to face the New Year. The heartache just never stops.'

Christine often finds herself thinking back over Anthony's life too, remembering the day he was born and how amazed she was by him. 'He weighed in at just 4 pounds 11 ounces, he was tiny. He spent the first three weeks of his life in an incubator and we were all worried sick over him, praying that he'd put on weight quickly so we could take him home. But he was a fighter and although he was six weeks' premature, he pulled through fine. I had been two days in labour and I was wrecked when he eventually arrived. But just to look down and see this tiny little bundle was fantastic.' Christine smiles when she remembers how spoiled he was when they finally got him home. Although Christine decided to move to London when Anthony was just a baby, she didn't let him forget his Dublin roots and, as he grew, Anthony talked about Ireland and its history with her and his grandparents. They came home once a year to visit family and these trips were always a highlight.

After Carmel and Louis moved back to Ireland, Louis became ill so Christine and Anthony moved home too. Anthony started school in Dublin and Christine was delighted that he made his Holy Communion in Ireland. But Anthony didn't settle in his new school and when his work started to suffer, Christine decided they should head back to London.

When Anthony came back to Dublin when he was 17, things were completely different. He settled very quickly. He went down to the FÁS office and picked plumbing as an apprenticeship. This surprised Christine because, as he was very good with computers, she had thought that that was the area he'd want to work in. But he chose plumbing and was happy with his choice.

'When I think back on him as a kid I have some funny memories,' Christine says. 'He loved reading, I'd read to him every night before he went to bed when he was really young. He wanted to be a private investigator when he started to get into the Sherlock Holmes books, he loved Harry Potter as well, but he also at one stage wanted to be a reporter, after doing some work experience with a newspaper in London. Then he got into music and I bought him decks and he wanted to be a DJ. He also wanted to be a stockbroker at one stage. When he was doing his work experience in school, he asked me did I know anyone who worked in stockbroking, so I organised it for him and on his first day there, he fell asleep on the computer. I thought it was hilarious. But despite all his hopes and dreams over the years, he seemed happy at the plumbing. He said to me that once he was finished and had his qualifications, he was going to travel. All those plans. It kills me that he will never get to do the things he wanted to do.'

Christine last saw her son three weeks before he was murdered at her cousin's 40th birthday party. He was in great form, laughing and dancing with all the family. She is glad that they had that night, where everyone had a good time and forgot their worries. But she is upset that she didn't see him during the next few weeks, though they did speak on the phone.

'I hadn't actually seen him for three weeks,' she says. 'That kills me. When we were chatting on the phone, he was telling me that he had lost his job and he was worried over Christmas. I kept telling him not to worry about buying presents. But he was genuinely worried over not being able to work. So, getting the odd job plumbing was great for him, not just for money but for his apprenticeship. The more experience he had on the job, the better for him in the long run.'

Christine is still battling to come to terms with what happened to her son on what should have been an ordinary day at work. She has visited the house where Anthony was shot—something many people find hard to believe—because she wanted to say a few prayers with a priest at the place he died. She says it was something she had to do—to see where he lost his life. But it didn't make her feel better. 'I felt sick to be honest that day but I'm glad I did it. I don't think I could ever do it again though. All the time I was wondering what it was like that morning. How was Anthony feeling when them fellas came in? I just pray that it was quick and that he didn't suffer too much. Because that's every parent's dread: that their child dies suffering. I just wish I could turn back time and have him back with me, see him laughing, having a few drinks with his pals. I just want to have him back to hug him, kiss him and tell him that I'll always love him.'

———

Another person who wishes they could turn back time, is retired detective inspector Brian Sherry, who led the investigation into Anthony's death. After 36 years in the force and having helped to solve many murders during the course of his career, he left the force in 2007 with one regret: that he wasn't able to secure a conviction for Anthony's brutal murder. It was the one case that he was hoping to solve before he retired.

'Over the years, I have worked on quite a considerable number of murders, but the most recent murder case that stands out in my mind is that of Marlo Hyland and young Anthony,' he says. 'They were the most memorable murders of recent times. Anthony was young and had a bright future ahead of him, he was a fine young individual. And what makes it more upsetting was that he was an only child. That was a very traumatic event for both his parents and for members of the gardaí who had to deal with it.'

Sherry says that many people think the guards are not affected by murders because they are used to attending horrific scenes but, he says, this is not the case. The guards are often the first people to arrive at a crime scene and it is they who have to deal with the reality of a brutal attack. He acknowledges that what the guards have to deal with has an impact. 'At the end of the day we are only human,' he says, 'and, in some cases, where the scene is particularly horrific, it could probably stay with you for the rest of your life.'

Although some memories fade with time, Sherry finds that certain images are difficult to forget. 'There are times when you might wake in the middle of the night and you realise that you have been dreaming about a crime scene, revisiting it in your head. It's normally the more horrific murders that tend to stick out in your mind. There's no real reason for one, more so than the other, but certain murders do stay there and affect you more. It is not only frustrating for the families of the victims when we fail to solve a case, it is also frustrating for the people who have put weeks, months and sometimes years into trying to nail these killers.'

For Brian, Anthony's youth and innocence are what make his murder stand out. It hurts him that no one was ever caught for the double murder and he hopes that one day that will change and those responsible will finally be brought to justice.

What the guards did discover from their investigation is that it appears that the two gunmen had a free run of the house—in other words, it was not unusual for them to be there. They could have walked in and out of the house all day and no one would have thought anything of it. No doubt, Anthony's presence took them by surprise. They hadn't planned on him being there. They would have seen Anthony's employer drive away as they waited but didn't realise he had anyone working with him. It is likely that the assailants didn't see Anthony get out of the van, on the passenger side, when they had first arrived that morning. They knew Hyland's niece had left the house as well and expected Hyland to answer the door when they called.

The guards say it is hard to know whether or not Anthony knew what was going to happen to him after Hyland had been shot. What everyone does hope is that his death was swift and that he didn't suffer the fear that could accompany this type of scenario.

Marlo Hyland was a completely different person to Anthony Campbell. He was a seasoned criminal and had received a number of death threats in the weeks and months before his murder. It was because of these threats that he had been moving around the Finglas and Cabra areas for a number of weeks, always trying to stay one step ahead of any threat.

The guards knew that Hyland had been staying at his niece's house for a few days before the murder and that he had fallen foul of other criminals. Whether or not he had decided to try to face them to negotiate his way out of the situation is something that they don't know, but it is one possibility. There had been a number of major drug seizures in the weeks prior to the murders and Hyland had been part of the deals. Because he had not been arrested, searched or caught with any drugs, the other criminals began to think that he might have been assisting the gardaí—and setting them up.

It is the sort of situation where it doesn't matter if there was any truth in the rumour or not, the thought was enough to create a situation within the criminal fraternity where Hyland's life became threatened.

Brian Sherry believes that Hyland had come to the conclusion that his life was in serious danger and that the consequences were inescapable at that particular time. He believes that Hyland was actively engaged in trying to negotiate with those who were in a position to prevent his murder. 'Life as a drug baron, or a person who is involved in the drug business, is relatively short and the reasons for this are varied,' says Sherry. 'It can be due to the use of the illegal drugs themselves, which can take an affect on their lives, but, generally speaking, it is simply a very dangerous business to become involved in, because while you are there and fighting your way to the top, you're surrounded by people who are assisting you, but who are also watching your position and waiting for you to make a mistake so that they can then move in and take over as the next 'drug baron', for want of a better expression.'

There have been a number of drug barons who have died relatively young. 'From my experience,' says Sherry, 'and from looking around, listening and gaining knowledge of other murders that have taken place in the city of Dublin and indeed around the country, the life expectancy certainly is a lot shorter than say the normal male.'

Sherry says that a main factor in young men becoming involved in crime is the lifestyle that goes with it. Young men become fascinated by the trappings of wealth and the other attractions associated come with this life. They often become involved in the drug business from an early age have a perception that it's easy to make quick money, with very little risk. The only real risk they think about is the possibility of a spell in prison—and at times it's better for them to be behind bars because it's a safer place to be than the streets.

The people who become involved in criminal gangs are mostly young men from a particular background—from corporation or council estates and those who are less well off in society. They are the ones who find this type of lifestyle attractive. They see others of a similar age to themselves with four-wheel-drive cars and they want the same luxuries. They see riches that are far beyond their expectations, the lifestyle becomes fascinating for them. They want what the others have, if not more. This seems to be why they become involved in the drugs trade and when they have become involved, it's very difficult for them to get out. They tend to struggle to get to the top of the tree rather than trying to get out. If other gang members see someone is trying to make a break, they could perceive that person as a threat to other members of the gang and so that person could be killed for that reason. Very often there is no way out.

Sherry believes that getting involved in the drugs trade in Ireland today is the equivalent to the situation in America in the 1970s and 1980s when young men got caught up in crime to make some easy money and then couldn't find a way out. 'You just can't go along to the rest of the gang, and say, "I want to get out, I've made my money and I want to get out of this and I want to go and invest in some other type of crime,"' he says. 'They would automatically see you as a liability, a threat to the rest of the group and that you could endanger their livelihoods and their lives. They see you as a weak link and the likelihood is that your life would be terminated.'

The criminal gangs normally live and deal in their own areas, where they have grown up and where they are most comfortable. They know the people around them and they know the other criminals operating in the area. Moving out of their comfort zone would leave them feeling isolated, so they tend to stay where they were brought up, though their houses tend to be very different to their neighbours'. 'They will have the latest technology,' says Sherry, 'the best of everything, be it a 42-inch television or state-of-the-art, American-style double fridges, all the trappings of wealth. They will have a good car in the drive, a top-of-the-range BMW or a four-wheel-drive jeep. These things are all status symbols. Very often, they would also have invested heavily in property abroad. Apart from expensive goods, they will also dress very well and will have carry a lot of disposable cash—often €2,000 or €3,000—and are not afraid to flash their money around, often to attract women.'

It is difficult to determine what turns some people into criminals. What makes some people evil enough to carry out a murder. Brian Sherry talks of the perception that the general public has that many of the young people who are involved in serious crime come from dysfunctional families, where the mother or father may have had alcohol problems or have abused drugs, or where there was a large family so attention couldn't be divided equally amongst all the children. In his opinion, there are definitely some cases where the young men had a certain level of deprivation growing up or an abusive, violent father or a mother who had left the home. 'There are a myriad of reasons why young people get involved in crime but the reality of it is everyone can be brought up and reared in difficult areas by good people. In most cases, it's simply down to how you choose to rear your family, the type of parents you are. No parent purposely rears their child to become a drug addict, a drug abuser or, for that matter, a drug baron. They don't rear them with a view to them becoming involved in crime. So there have to be a number of reasons as to why young people become involved in crime. People say that there's a definite link between social background and crime, but not every child from this background grows up to become a criminal. And some of these guys who do go down that road are very clever.'

Sherry knows that the general public thinks that the rate of success in solving gangland crime is low, but says there are a number of reasons for this. A main reason is that gang members remain silent when they are arrested. They are brought up to believe that if you are caught, you don't talk to the police, you don't give them any information and you don't talk to anyone about what you or your colleagues are doing. And it's very hard for the gardaí to breech that sort of mindset.

'I have had experiences where young criminals come in and they would literally sit for the full period of their detention in an inter-view room, just staring at the floor, refusing to acknowledge their name let alone their existence,' says Sherry. 'That said, there have been successes and the gardaí are continuing to work on these cases and they put in a lot of resources to crack these crimes.'

This attitude means that the guards have to rely on specific evidence, on fingerprint or forensic evidence or the evidence of a witness, otherwise it becomes difficult to connect the criminals to a murder or any serious crime.

There are other ways of defeating these gangs. A main resource assisting the gardaí is the Criminal Assets Bureau (CAB), which takes money from those involved in crime in the form of the pro-ceeds of their crimes. This negates one of the main attractions to young men who are thinking of becoming involved. They start to think that it isn't worth their while to commit a crime or have money in their possession. Today, CAB is targeting smaller groups of criminals who are involved in the areas where crime or drugs are more prevalent.

However, there are other areas that could be changed to help the gardaí and organisations like CAB have more success against the drug gangs. Brian Sherry believes that the law needs to be re-addressed in relation to 'the right to silence' for criminals, where-by they don't have to answer questions if their answers would incriminate them. He has serious concerns about this particular aspect of the law and says that many innocent people are worried by it. 'But,' he says, 'very few innocent people who are supposed to be involved in criminal gangs are arrested and asked to account for their movements or account for their wealth or asked to account for where they were on Saturday night when the murder was committed. Very few innocent people find themselves in this position throughout their lifetime.'

He believes very strongly that the general public needs to understand the situation fully. 'People have to realise this is a war and we need to get the people who are responsible for this mayhem because they are bringing the rest of this country down. The number of murders that have been committed by these people is beyond belief.'

People are undoubtedly shocked when an innocent person is murdered, simply because they were in the wrong place at the wrong time. But when the news reports have been read, they go back to their lives, far removed from this criminal underworld. But, as Sherry points out, when a criminal is murdered the fallout is just the same as when an innocent person is killed, his parents, his brothers, his sisters, his wider family, his friends all have to deal with the murder. Many of these people have never been involved in crime. Often the general public will be blasé when they hear about the death of a drug dealer, wondering who cares. To many, the death of a criminal, especially a drug dealer, is not something to be mourned—it is one less villain to worry about—but every young person who is murdered has a family. 'This attitude is a reflection on our society,' Sherry says, 'because, as I've often said, no mother sends their child out to commit crime. No mother sends their child out to commit murder. I'm a firm believer in that, I've yet to meet the mother who does.'

In recent years, it has become apparent to Brian Sherry and to other observers that most of the gangland hits have been very well planned, meticulously orchestrated from start to finish. The assassins make every effort to cover every single track so that they don't unwittingly give the guards any leads and bring them to their doorsteps.

'The money and power associated with each and every execution is just too much to gamble with,' he says. These hits don't just happen accidentally. They're planned over a period of time. There may, in fact, be several attempts to get it right before the actual murder takes place. There's a lot of logistics involved in getting the firearm, getting transport, getting safe houses and I suppose ultimately the person who is prepared to pull the trigger and do the deed. Not a lot of people out there are prepared to take on a gangland figure and shoot them. They are very few and far between.'

However, they are sometimes prepared to commit a murder for a relatively small amount of money. This is because there are other factors motivating them. People who were a close ally of the murder victim are approached by other criminals—either from their own gang or another gang—and are offered not only money but the promise of elevation within the gang structure. This is often a main reason for carrying out a murder and, in recent times, there has been a definite trend towards committing serious crimes for elevation within the gang structure.

There are different types of hitmen operating in Ireland, though, to Sherry, the general public is not aware of the numbers that exist here. He says people believe that these men are brought in from the UK or Eastern Europe to carry out an execution, but the reality is far different. There are quite a number of Irish people who are prepared to commit murder for as little as €2,000 or €3,000, depending on the type of individual who is to be targeted and type of threat they pose to either a gang or their position within the gang. These hitmen may be considered to be at the lower end of the scale. They would often be involved in drugs themselves and would commit a serious crime for the simple reason that, when they have finished, they are guaranteed a fix that would keep them going for the next couple of weeks or months. This is the most common type of hitman. However, Ireland has a legacy of political unrest and violence. Because of the success of the peace process, the people who were involved in terrorism—in murdering people—now find themselves redundant. It is very hard for them to change and to stop what they were doing and find regular employment. For some of those who were involved in the paramilitary organisations, it is easier to offer their services to the criminal gangs—though their experience and ruthlessness comes at a price. These men are cold-blooded killers and will kill for money alone.

'There are people out there who put bread on their table by killing,' says Sherry, 'and these people would also be involved in other serious crime, like the distribution of drugs themselves. They would be involved on the periphery of that or on major bank robberies or cash in transit robberies, that type of crime. These people would consider it simply as a 'favour' for another criminal.'

Both types of hitman active in Ireland like to get close to their victim, very close. The firearm they use is generally small range, such as a handgun or a sawn-off shotgun. To use these weapons, they have to get near to their target and, in most cases that the guards have investigated, the victim is lured to the site of the hit by someone who is close to them, someone they trust. The handgun that is generally used is a Glock 9mm, it is the sort of weapon that, when used, is going to kill.

From his own experience, Brian Sherry has seen how these mostly self-trained assassins will shoot their victim in the chest first before following up with a shot to the head. In most cases, it is the head shot that proves fatal. 'But that's the type of individual that you're talking about,' he says. 'These are not just people who will go up with their hand shaking as they hold a gun or be worried about other individuals there who might be armed. They fear no one. These are people who have used firearms before and who are quite capable of murder, in fact murder doesn't create any problem for them.'

Even though many of these men are untrained, there is a lot of investigative evidence to suggest that some of them are making regular trips to Eastern Europe where they practise with various types of weapon to perfect their shot. They may also have travelled to the US and South America to use the ranges there. They are seasoned gunmen, proficient in the use of firearms and who understand everything about their weapon—its accuracy, calibre and the distance required to make a successful hit.

There is no doubt that these hitmen are very dangerous people and need to be stopped. But the biggest problem the gardaí face is gathering enough evidence that will link the hitmen beyond doubt to a crime—as well as finding witnesses who are prepared to stand up in a court of law and say what they have seen. Brian Sherry knows it is a huge undertaking for someone to agree to be a witness, but the guards cannot work in isolation without the help of the public. 'Without that help,' he says, 'our hands are tied.'

02 GUNNED DOWN AT A HOUSE PARTY

DONNA CLEARY

When Clayton Cleary, who is just five years old, asks his nanny, 'When is Mammy coming home?', it breaks her heart. Although this beautiful blond, football-mad, little boy knows that his mother is 'up with Holy God in Heaven', he's still too young to understand that he'll never see her again.

Clayton was only three when his vivacious, fun-loving mother was gunned down by a gang of local thugs, who started shooting because they had been refused entry to a house party in Coolock on the northside of Dublin.

Donna Cleary, from Castlekevin Road in Coolock, was an innocent victim brutally killed in an Ireland that seems to have lost control of gun crime.

The evening of 4 March 2006 started off like any other Saturday night for Donna. She had arranged for her big brother, Keith, to mind Clayton so that she could go to a birthday party being held for her friend, Edel Murtagh, at the Inis Fail GAA Club in Balgriffin. The plan was for a main party to be at the club and then for a few friends to go back to Edel's mother's house at Adare Green in Coolock for a few drinks and a bit of a singsong.

Donna was looking forward to the night out and, as usual, Kathleen, her mother, was called on for a bit of advice on what to wear. Kathleen and Donna had a great relationship, more like friends than mother and daughter. Donna always loved to hear what her mother thought about how she looked when she headed out for a night and Kathleen loved to give her daughter advice.

And that night was no different.

Kathleen remembers the build-up to the party very well. 'Donna had no babysitter that evening, so she got her brother to mind Clayton. I knew the party was coming up but I was going out myself that night with my sisters. She was all excited about going to the party, she was after buying a new dress. Before she went out, she said to me, "Mam will I wear shoes or boots with the dress?" It was a lovely jumper dress with hot pants underneath, so I told her to wear the shoes. And then she said, "Won't you leave out a key for me?" And I told her I would. And that was that. The last time we spoke. That night our lives were destroyed forever. The person who killed our daughter not only ruined our lives, but took a mammy away from a little three-year-old boy.'

Donna meant everything to her parents, Peter and Kathleen. Their only daughter, she was a younger sister for her two older brothers, Glen and Keith. Kathleen remembers that the day Donna was born, they felt that their family was finally complete. Photographs all around their house show a lovely smiling little girl who obviously loved playing up for the camera as she posed for shots.

'She was a gorgeous little thing,' says Kathleen. 'She was very chubby and looked like her dad. And I loved having her around the house. As she grew older, she was a handful at times and we had to keep her on a tight rein, the usual thing with teenagers. We had to show her who was boss because she was very headstrong. Little things like she hated wearing the school coat. The trouble I used to have getting her to put it on.'

Donna went to her local school, St John of God on Kilmore Road. Her bubbly personality attracted everyone she met and she had a large circle of friends both at school and outside.

'It was different rearing a girl after two boys to be honest and I always worried about her,' Kathleen says. 'I worried about them all, but I worried more about Donna because she was a girl. Your biggest worry as your kids are growing up today is drugs and I always prayed that none of them would get involved in drugs. But they were all good kids.'

Peter and Kathleen have great memories of Donna as a young girl. 'When she was much younger she was very clingy,' says Peter. 'No matter where I went, Donna would always be stuck on me leg. If I was going out on the bike, she'd be up like a light with me, jump onto the handlebars and wherever I was going on the bike she'd be with me. She was the apple of my eye, she was a little cracker. I get very emotional when I talk about her. A daughter means everything in the world to a father. And I'd give up every-thing I have in this life to have her back. She was with me when I went to the pigeon club and even when I ran the football club. She'd come down to the training sessions with me. She was my little shadow. I think nearly everybody knew her.'

Kathleen agrees. 'Even though myself and Donna got on great, she was definitely a daddy's girl. She loved helping her da out with the pigeons in the back garden. Peter has racing pigeons and Donna loved to go out the back to help him out as soon as she came in from school. They were very close. She went everywhere with him. She'd come in from school and drop the schoolbag and straight out to her da out the back. She did very well at school but her favourite subject was art. And when she was in school, she worked at night-time in the catering business for a few bob. Her other love was beauty. She loved dressing up herself, doing her make-up and she loved fashion. And her dream was to work as a beautician.'

Donna's dream to work as a beautician was one that she was close to realising. For the few months before she was killed, Donna had headed off to a beauty course every Saturday morning. Her mother would mind Clayton for the day and he would either play on the street with his pals or go shopping with his nanny. Kathleen was happy to take care of her grandson because she knew that Donna was doing everything she could to educate herself to make a better life for herself and her little boy.

'I remember when she eventually finished her course she came in with a big bunch of flowers to thank me. That was what she was like, very loving. She had just signed up for a nail course as well, which would have meant that she could finally go to work as a beautician full-time, her dream job, but that will never happen now. Her dream is gone. It's horrible to think that she had all these plans and now they're all gone.'

——

Edel Murtagh will never forget her 40th birthday party—but for all the wrong reasons. It was a landmark birthday and she had been deciding on what to do for two years. In the end, she chose to go to a club at Inis Fail GAA, with all her girl friends and then just her family and some close friends would go back to her mother's house to finish the evening.

'It was a good night at the club, up until we saw these fellas in the corner of the room. They had approached my sister and asked her if they could come back to the party in the house, but she said no to them. Then, one of them came over to me and I told him that they couldn't come back. I said, "I don't even know you. You've had a good night here so just leave it and go home lads." I thought that was it. But when I got back to my mother's house, they had already been there and had smashed flowerpots against the windows when my sister turned them away. Cars were starting to pull up at the house as friends arrived, but I had decided that the party wasn't going to go ahead because of what had happened, so I walked out to tell everyone. And then these fellas, the same ones, came around the corner in a car, pulled up, stepped out and started shooting.'

In the panic that followed, where people were screaming and running to get out of the way, Edel found herself rooted to the ground with fear, unable to move and unable to comprehend what was happening.

'People were shouting, "They have a gun, they have a gun, they have a gun,"' she remembers, 'but I didn't know what to do. It was the girls' screaming that brought me back to reality. I had been standing there in shock. I ran into the house and I saw Donna. She was snow white and everyone was saying, "She's hurt, she's hurt." Donna was trying to stay standing, then, all of a sudden, she hit the ground and my sister-in-law, Olivia, was giving her CPR on the floor.'

The scene was mayhem, with people still screaming and shouting, uncertain about what had happened. There was so much chaos that some people in the house didn't know that Donna had been shot. It had all happened with frightening speed. To those near her in the house, it became apparent within a matter of minutes that Donna had a fight on her hands if she was to survive.

'I was trying to push everybody back to get a space for her and to get some air into the room,' says Edel. 'But everyone was screaming. I was pushing everybody back from around Donna because Olivia was working on her, trying to help her. I went down on my hands and knees and I put my hand over her wound, where the bullet had gone in. I don't know why I did that, but I put my hand over her wound until the ambulance came. It was very frightening.'

As they all waited for the ambulance to arrive, Donna's thoughts were with her young son, and she repeatedly called his name. Friends remember how she just seemed to want Clayton with her. 'It was horrible,' remembers Edel. 'She was calling her son's name. I'd say she knew it was serious. Another friend, Leanne, was down beside her saying, "Hold on, Donna. Think of Clayton. Hold on and think of your mam and dad." Donna's face was very frightened, it was a grey colour and you could see the pain there. She had this gaunt look that I can't really describe. It was the first time I ever experienced anything like it. Everyone was very upset and I knew when I looked at her that she wasn't going to make it. I saw the life leaving her.'

In the days that followed Donna's death, the events surrounding the shooting became clearer.

A group of friends, including Donna, were already at the house, waiting outside for Edel to arrive, when the gang returned. When the men started throwing plant pots at the windows, the party-goers all ran inside the house. As the friends sat in the front room, discussing what had happened, Donna and a few others went just outside the front door to start tidying up the broken pots. As they were clearing up the mess, the gang returned. Donna was running inside to warn everyone that the thugs were back when they started shooting.

'I didn't know what was going on, I didn't hear anything,' remembers Stacey Manning, another of Donna's friends. 'My boyfriend actually had to drag me and push me to the floor. I was lying on the floor and Donna was just over by my feet. At that stage, I didn't know she'd been shot. Then people started shouting, calling out that Donna was hit. When I realised what had happened, I just started screaming, trying to get over to her, people were just dragging me out of the room and I had to be held down in the sitting room. I couldn't get near her. People were just trying to get everyone out of the way so they could see if she was OK. There were only two or three people with her, the rest of us were kept in the sitting room. I didn't even know where she had been shot. Leanne was the calmest because she was outside when it happened, so she came in to see if Donna was OK.'

When the ambulance had taken Donna to Beaumont Hospital, the gardaí asked everyone to stay in the house to make statements, but everyone there wanted to go to the hospital to see if Donna was OK. In the end, the gardaí took their names and addresses and people started calling taxis to go to Beaumont.

Although those who had comforted Donna whilst she waited for the ambulance knew her condition was serious, others didn't fully understand what had happened and thought Donna would be OK. Stacey remembers staying at the hospital for about an hour and a half, before she decided to go home because she had a bad headache. 'I asked my friends to ring me and let me know how she was and I headed home. I honestly thought she was going to be all right. I was just walking up the steps of the hospital when I heard two friends screaming. I turned to my boyfriend and said, "She's not?" and he said to me, "She's gone, she's gone." I was screaming and I ran down the stairs to where my two friends were and the two of them said that she had gone. We all just started crying and hugging each other. We couldn't believe it.'

Donna died from massive internal injuries. When she was shot, the bullet had pierced the side of her rib cage and had punctured her lung.

——

To everyone who knew her, Donna was a beautiful, caring, friendly girl, with a wonderful laugh and a sunshine personality.

She loved parties and going out at the weekends with her girl friends and she loved to have a bit of craic. But the light of her life was her son, Clayton. Stacey remembers what a great mother Donna was and how excited she was to be getting her own house for herself and Clayton. 'She had been doing her beautician's course and she used all of us as guinea pigs. We were all getting freebies, eyebrow waxing, facials, the works. We loved it. She was a great friend and would do anything for you. She was just a great person to be around. You'd never feel bored around her and she'd always make you laugh. She'd make something out of nothing just to put a smile on your face.

'I have lots of good memories of Donna. If you were getting into trouble or anything in school and you were trying to keep a serious face, she'd always be poking or prodding you to make you laugh, to get you into more trouble. She just couldn't keep still or keep a straight face. She was always happy and making us laugh. If you were sad, she made you laugh. If you were in trouble, she made you laugh. No matter what, she just could not be serious, that's what we all loved about Donna, she was just mad. It's the only word I could use to describe her. She loved dressing up, getting her hair done and doing her make up and I think she would have made a great beautician. If they hadn't taken her life from her.

'When she became pregnant with Clayton she was very nervous about being a single mum, but she was also really looking forward to his birth. When he arrived she was absolutely delighted. She was so happy to be a mammy. But she'll never get to see her little boy make his Holy Communion or go out on his first real date with a girl. It's all been taken away from her.'

For Kathleen and Peter, Clayton is a connection to Donna whom they cherish. He constantly brings up her name because he wants his mother to come home. On Clayton's fifth birthday, he got a little helium balloon with Santa Claus on it and Peter and Kathleen put a message on it saying, 'With love from Clayton.' They let it go and it floated up into the sky. 'Clayton says his mammy is with Holy God,' says Peter. He was delighted. He thinks it's gone up to his mammy. Even the other day he said to Kathleen, "She's gone a long time, when is she coming back? We'll have to get her clothes. How is she going to get clothes, new clothes up there?"' The little comments he makes and the questions he asks tear Kathleen and Peter apart. Both in their sixties, this couple could never have imagined that they would be raising their grand-child on their own without his mother around. No one could have imagined that life would be so cruel and deal them such a severe blow. An ordinary couple never previously affected by crime of any sort, they have found themselves with no option but to bring up Clayton in the house he has always known as home.

But it isn't always easy to raise a feisty boy, as both grandparents know only too well.

'I'm at the stage now where I know I have to get on with it,' says Kathleen. 'Sometimes, it's hard, though, for example when Clayton is tired and he isn't getting his own way and he cries for his mammy. It's very hard though when all you have left are memories. And the house feels very empty with Donna no longer around. There's a dead feeling in it.'

Today, Clayton is five, full of life and always on the go. Peter and Kathleen give him all the love they have, but it is hard for them. As Kathleen says, they don't have the same energy as they did when they were raising their our own children. Clayton reminds Kathleen of Donna in many ways. When he is running around, Kathleen remembers how Donna ran exactly the same way, he also has a bit of a temper just like she did. Donna and Clayton's father had separated before Donna was killed, and Clayton rarely saw him, leaving Donna to bring him up alone. 'We have to do our best for him,' Kathleen says. 'Having him with us is like having a piece of Donna still here. But Clayton has to go through his whole life now without his mammy. When he sees a blonde lady, he looks round thinking, Is it my mammy? When he was four, someone gave him a red car with a blonde woman figure inside and he said, "There's my ma in the car." Things like that are heartbreaking for us. But we just have to go on. He is a little handful but I know that Donna would be so proud of him because he has started school and he's doing very well. He loves playing football and bowling and he loves it when I go out onto the road to watch him on his bike. Luckily I still have a little bit of energy that I can kind of keep going.'

'Sometimes, when you come home and you're knackered it's very hard,' Peter agrees, 'but you'd just sit down and hold him and hug him. He loves the night-time when he gets into his pyjamas and jumps on to me lap and the first thing he says is, "Do incey wincey spider." The minute I hear those words, I know he's going to sleep because he just lies down and I'll tickle his back for him and he's gone.

'At the moment, for myself and Kathleen, it's like a whole new world starting again. 'We've reared the two sons and Donna and we thought that when the family was reared up, we'd have been able to go off and have holidays, the usual and get the grandchildren for a visit at the weekend. Now we have Clayton all the time and it's only through his Auntie Sharon taking him some weekends that we have a break and we get out. Kathleen only does three days a week now in work and I do five days but we only do four hours a day. Kathleen is in work at eight o'clock and I get up when she leaves, get Clayton ready, get him to school and go to work at one o'clock. When Kathleen finishes she picks him up from school at half one. So our whole lives have been turned around again and we have had to change completely, at a time when, in fact, we should be relaxing and enjoying our lives. I'd rather little Clayton have his mother around him, like other children, but to me he is part of Donna. He has her little smile and you can nearly see Donna in him. He's a great little kid. But at our age it can be hard. But I wouldn't change him for the world. He keeps us going, but you do need an outlet.

'Kathleen goes to line dancing and I'll sit in with Clayton, because I don't have the heart to go out much at all. But Kathleen needs to get a break. We have to get on with life but we will never forget what happened. How can you? We reared our daughter from a baby until she was 22 and we thought she'd be grand, but you just never know what's around the corner.'

Their love for Clayton doesn't make the loss of their daughter easier to bear. They are still grieving and dealing with the fact that Donna is never going to walk through their door again. She is still the first thought in Kathleen's mind in the morning and her last thought every night. 'I think she would be happy with how we are looking after Clayton. Shortly after she died, I remember being in the kitchen and I could feel her there. I knew she was there and I could feel her telling me to get out there and enjoy myself. I really believe she was there with me that day and that's a comfort. Peter and I lean on each other all the time. It's the only way we can get through. Unless you have lost someone like this you could never imagine how it devastates you. It's not like losing a child in a car crash or through cancer, it's something that no one could ever imagine because you see it on the television but you never think in a million years that it could happen to you.'

Peter still remembers the last time he saw his little girl as she got ready to go out for the evening. 'I remember I saw Donna around six o'clock that night. She had arranged for my son, Keith, to mind Clayton. I was sat in the armchair and she went upstairs with her ma to get ready. I fell asleep in the chair and when I woke up she had gone, sneaked out the door. And that was it. The last time I saw her in the house. People say that time is a healer but no one knows what it's like unless it's happened to them.'

On the night Donna died, Peter and Kathleen sat for a long 45 minutes, waiting to hear how their daughter was doing. They weren't allowed in to see her because the doctors were working, trying to save her. Finally, they were told that she was stable and would be moved to the Mater Hospital where there was a surgeon who could help her. Feeling relieved, they waited to be told when Donna would be moved. But the relief was short lived and, not long after, the doctors told them that Donna had gone into shock and had died.

'We just couldn't believe this was happening,' remembers Kathleen. 'We had been able to see Donna's head as they worked on her so we thought she was going to be fine, we never expected her to die. But we know that the doctors did all they could for her. It really hurt us that we never got to talk to her. We know that in the ambulance she was looking for Clayton so I think she knew how serious it was. I remember after they told us just sitting in the hospital with Peter on one side crying, my son, Glen, on the other side and then my other son, Keith, came up and we were all just inconsolable.'

Donna's family were told she had died from a gunshot wound to the chest. They found it very hard to stay calm, especially Donna's brothers, this was because they knew exactly who had killed her. A lot of people at the party, including Donna, would have known those who attacked the house. Donna knew one of the men very well and had been a good friend to him. Donna's family find his part in her death hard to accept. This particular attacker was the only one brought to court and Donna's friends shouted at him tell the truth, for Donna's sake. But all those suspected of the attack have walked free. This is something that is very hard for Donna's family and friends to come to terms with. 'Even Clayton when he saw a photo of the man in the papers at the time said, "That's Mammy's friend,"' remembers Kathleen. 'In fact, he is now out of the country. It's very hard knowing that no one is paying the price for taking my daughter's life. It's just horrible to think that they are all walking about and Donna is dead. Where is the justice in that?'

What Kathleen and Peter now want more than anything is justice for Donna and for Clayton and the day someone is found guilty of her murder cannot come quickly enough.

Peter Cleary is heartbroken at the loss of his little girl and has suffered with severe health problems since she was killed. The one thing he is grateful for is that no one else was shot that night.' There could have been six or seven people killed,' he says. 'It would have been horrendous.' This sense of relief that no one else was killed is also felt by those who were at the house. Edel remembers finding bullet holes all over the front of the house over the following days. 'I know one went into the window frame, another went into a wall and others were found in the garden. They just opened fire and were shooting literally anywhere. Even the gardaí can't believe more people weren't killed. Unfortunately, it was poor Donna who lost her life, but it could have been many more.'

But for those left behind, it's painful to move on. 'I go around with a smile on me face all the time,' Peter says, 'but inside it's killing me. But you have to keep going for Clayton's sake. Kathleen and Donna were so friendly, pals they were. I've often said to Kathleen, "If I could take Donna's place, I would." Just to bring her back for her—because I know I'm broke up inside but Kathleen is destroyed. There's nights when we're out and she'd just break down. But that's something we've to live with.

'When we got to the hospital, they were operating on Donna and the door of the room was open a bit and that was my last sighting of Donna, seeing her kicking her legs about, literally fighting for her life. She was awake and kicking about. Then the policeman came over and told us that we couldn't see her and the doctor closed the door and that was it. But we genuinely thought she'd be fine, especially when they said that she was stable. When the man came out and brought myself, Kathleen and my two sons into a room and said she had died, all hell broke loose. It was a nightmare. Everybody was screaming and roaring and crying and just stunned. They had to sedate me because I was uncontrollable. I mean she went to a party, the apple of my eye, and they killed her. At a party! I could have killed someone that night if they hadn't given me something to calm me down.

'The doctors said Donna died from one shot through her chest. I think it came through the side of her chest and punctured her lungs and they were trying to pump the blood out because too much blood went into her lungs, but it was just too severe. I didn't even recognise her when they brought us in to see her because her face was bloated out with fluids and even the day when we were in the mortuary, when they had her laid out, she didn't look like the same lovely girl we knew. My little girl always had a smile on her face, a big smile that everyone talked about who knew her. She was no angel but she'd melt you with that smile and there she was lying there with no smile, no heart-melting smile, just lying there dead.'

———

For many people, but especially her family and friends, Donna's death has changed their perspective on how they live and how they view their city. There is a real fear now. The rows and pushing that would often go with a night out and which were considered normal after a few drinks are feared. Not knowing how someone will react if you bump into them or if someone will take offence at an innocent remark has become the norm.

'It has affected everyone,' says Edel. 'Mr and Mrs Cleary, all Donna's friends. It's ricocheted across the whole of Kilmore, nobody can believe it actually happened here.'

'Everything is changing,' says Stacey. 'It's not fist fights anymore, it's guns, knives and it's just ridiculous how people don't seem to care anymore. If you look at somebody wrong, you don't know what you're in for when you walk outside. Anything could happen to you. You just try and keep away from all that.'

Both Stacey and Edel are nervous when they go out at night. They still go out with their friends to clubs, but instead of hanging around town or going into the local chipper at the end of the night, they prefer to head straight home, just in case a fight breaks out on a street or in a bar.

'When we leave a nightclub now we just head straight home, whereas before we would stand around talking to people that we knew,' says Stacey. 'We can't do that anymore because anything can happen when the nightclub closes and you don't know who's around you and what they could do.'

A night out will never be the same again for any of Donna's close friends—life will never be the same. They have spoken of their fears for the future, for what their own children will face as they grow up in Ireland's climate of drink, drugs and guns. 'Before any of this happened,' Stacey says, 'I didn't really pay much attention but since Donna was killed, you hear of someone else being murdered every other week. Because today people are just going around with guns shooting innocent people for no reason at all. Innocent people are being caught in the crossfire. I'd be terrified to let my kids out, even in their own garden. It's just all gone mad.'

Edel is also scared about the future and regularly has nightmares about the night her young friend was shot. She is very cautious about where she goes and finds that she is always looking to see who's around her. She has become very nervous because she never thought anything like this could ever happen to her. 'You'd read about it in places like America, but I never thought it could happen in Dublin, and in my own ma's house, it's very scary. I wish I had never had the party. I always think to myself if I hadn't had the party, Donna would still be alive. It has really affected me. I'm not mad about parties anymore. I have nightmares all the time, reliving what happened.'

There is a sense that Donna's murder brought her friends closer together and they stayed close. The Christmas after her death, Donna's friends got together for an evening to talk about that night nine months earlier and how they had all been devastated by what had happened.

Along with the devastation and shock and the need to rebuild their lives, there is anger amongst Donna's friends that no one has been tried for her death.

'I don't think the government do enough to people who take other people's lives,' says Stacey. 'They are harder on people who rob banks or deal drugs than they are on those who murder innocent people. It's ridiculous that nothing can be done to get these fellas, just because of one or two technical things. It's not fair on

Donna's family. They need to see justice done. Her name still comes up in the newspapers every now and then but that's not enough. Something needs to be done and somebody needs to be brought to justice for taking her life. It's the only way that Peter and Kathleen, or any of us, are going to be able to move on. I just hope that one day someone will be charged. It's no use saying that the gardaí might get them for some other small crime—something not related to Donna's murder—someone has to be charged and put in jail for taking her life. Then maybe we could all move on knowing that Donna got some sort of justice. There will come a time when she will just be forgotten about by the public and I dread that. The whole thing, the whole injustice of it, really makes me angry.'

———

Peter Cleary finds it difficult to think of those who killed his daughter. He doesn't understand how they could do what they did or what type of people they are. Even knowing details of what happened that night leaves him sad and anxious.

'One of the witnesses said that the main fella was standing there just firing, and every time he shot the gun, it jolted and it just kept jolting and he moved along in a line across the house with the gun. The bullet that killed Donna shot down the hall, ricocheted and shot back and got Donna in the chest. But when she fell to the ground, her friends thought she was messing, lying on the ground. When they went to lift her up, they saw all the blood on their hands and they started screaming for someone to get an ambulance.

'People talk about justice, and I know justice won't bring her back, and it doesn't cure everything, but at least it would give me some peace of mind that these people were brought to task for it,' he says. 'But to be let just walk away. These people are still out there on the streets, how many more innocent people have to die until there's justice?'

Peter feels there is a fundamental problem with the way justice is dealt with in Ireland, he says it is 'all backwards'. 'They're sending out the wrong vibes to people, the wrong messages are going out there. There's innocent people getting killed and there's nothing being done about it. I've always maintained that I'm not letting Donna's death get pushed under the carpet and forgotten about. There's no way. And I'll fight to the bitter end until I get some sort of justice, someone has to be held responsible for her death.'

Peter and Kathleen are bewildered by what has happened to the men suspected of killing their daughter. They can't understand why the DPP never brought the case to court, given that there are witnesses from the evening who picked out the men in lineouts. For Peter, this should be enough evidence to bring a case to court. He doesn't understand what more is needed. He has read about other cases, where people have been convicted when there were no witnesses, and yet when people have declared that they saw these men there on the night, nothing happens. The DPP can't bring a case. It is something he can't grasp.

'There are more than 40 people putting the men responsible in the Inis Fail GAA Club and at the house throwing the flowerpots— and they don't get charged. They don't even get charged with malicious damage to the house. If I went out and broke someone's window there tonight, they'd soon have me in court and they'd lock me up. This is a murder.'

The situation makes Peter angry. The injustice of having Donna taken away from them, at Clayton having to grow up without his mother and at nobody being held responsible for what happened.

Peter believes the government has been giving the wrong message when it comes to murder. He thinks the gardaí should be given more powers to arrest and hold suspects. He also feels that the families of victims should be kept up to date on the case on a weekly or monthly basis when possible.

———

After the initial attack on the house that night nobody believed for one moment that those men would come back with a gun. But Ireland has changed and, today, it seems anything can happen.

'People say I'm bitter,' says Peter, 'but that's not the word. I wouldn't like to say how I feel because I wouldn't lower myself to that level. I've reared a nice family and they should be allowed go out and enjoy themselves without any fear. I always thank God that my children grew up straight. I had no problems with them. They weren't angels, they all done things they shouldn't have done over the years, even Donna wasn't an angel, but we did our best with them. I suppose you worry that the boys will get into trouble, get into fights, but you don't expect something like this to happen to a girl. We used to live in a comfort zone, nobody touched my family or our home, and I didn't really care what happened in the outside world, but when it happened to Donna, it changed things. When it happens to you, you realise just how bad things have gone here in Dublin. No one cares when the scumbags are killed, let them kill one another as far as I'm concerned, but when it's innocent people, then we have a problem. All I can do now is look back on the last few words I had with my daughter that day; my last memories of her. You don't ever think when your child is 22 years old that you have to remember every conversation you have with them, because you may never see them again, but that's how it is now. No one is safe.

'When you go out the front door nobody knows what's going to happen, when it's your children who have gone out, it's harder. That's the way Dublin has gone now. You might not be able to stop something bad happening to them. Every parent out there will tell you that when their daughters or their sons walk in through the door at night, there's a sense of relief. You'll sit there waiting for them and as soon as the front door opens and they're home, you'll relax. But if you can't walk the streets of Dublin what are we all going to do? Stay in our houses and not go out?'

Everything has changed for Kathleen and Peter since that night, their whole lives have been turned upside down. 'I don't have the heart I used to have,' says Peter. 'We go out and have a couple of pints, although even that's rare, but I haven't even got the heart at times to get up and dance because something tells me that if I start jumping and dancing around, I've forgotten about Donna. And I'd sit there and let Kathleen get up to dance, but I just can't get up.'

Peter feels the same about other areas of his life. He finds it difficult to raise pigeons any more as this was something he used to do with Donna. He feels the interest has gone for everything in life. Even though it's been two years since Donna died, people still come up and talk to Peter about it, what happened will never leave him. The main focus he has now is Clayton, to do the best for his young grandson, for Donna's sake. He thinks it will become harder as Clayton gets older but Peter trusts in God that Clayton will come out the other side all right. 'If he grows up like his uncles he'll be a good one, that's the best we can look for.'

One thing that Peter is certain about is that Clayton won't be allowed near drugs or anything like them as he gets older. He feels that people don't really understand the harm that drugs can cause. 'After the initial buzz, they feel nothing—or worse than nothing,' he says. He believes that drugs are at the heart of a lot of the gun and crime problems Ireland has and thinks the law needs to be tougher on dealers—that their movements should be monitored at all times to avoid more deaths.

Peter knows how hard it was for Donna, as a single mother, to raise Clayton, but, now, he is so grateful that God gifted her with the little boy who is a living connection to her.

'I remember when she came in and told me that she was pregnant, she was only 19. She was terrified. Like most young people who get pregnant before they get married, she didn't want to tell her da, but I said to her it would be grand and once the baby was healthy that was all that mattered. From the time she was a child, Donna loved babies and having Clayton was the best thing that happened to her. She brought him everywhere with her and she idolised him. And I'm proud of her for how she coped and how she did her best for her little boy.'

All Peter and Kathleen have now are memories of their little girl. They feel lucky because they are such great memories of a smiling, bubbly girl. 'I remember the day she passed her driving test and how happy she was when she told me. That will always sit in my head,' says Peter. 'She got into the car and drove down to her old school and went in the front gate and started beeping her horn and waving at the teacher, because she was a demon in school. She was able to stand up for herself no bother. At times, she used to ring up and say, "Da, I'm in trouble in school with the headmaster," and I'd have to go down. But I thought it was very funny that she drove down to the school that day and started beeping the horn because that was her way of saying, I came to something, I came to something, she was delighted with herself. I'll always have her memories, I'll never lose them.

'There's not a day, not a day goes by, that I don't expect her to come through the front door. If I see a black car with a blondey girl in it, my head turns, a natural reflex. All of a sudden I'd think there she is and then I realise it's not her.

'Her outlook on life was brilliant, and she had a great brain in her head, she knew exactly what she wanted and she was heading in the right direction. Her pride and joy were Clayton and her car. She always used to say, "Someday I'm going to have a BMW!" She had the money for it because she saved, she'd done her beautician's course and she had done nixers left right and centre to make a few bob extra and she put all her money away. She had put in for an affordable house and had her money stacked away for it. She was buying little pots and pans and the whole lot, she had them all under the bed. She was cute. She had her life set out but unfortunately life didn't pan out the way it should have.'

Peter and Kathleen are still trying to hold on to every little memory they have of Donna. They are both determined to keep her alive in their hearts and their home. They have kept her bedroom exactly how she left it and it is now where Clayton sleeps. Peter stays with him because Clayton sometimes wakes up during the night. They've added a few photographs of Donna because Clayton is always asking about her.

They take Clayton to Donna's grave a lot, every second week if possible. They call it his mammy's secret garden and he loves going to visit her. When they arrive, Clayton knows immediately where to go and heads straight over to her grave and kisses his mother's photograph on the headstone.

As Clayton has become older, he has become more curious about Donna and what happened to her. 'It's very hard to explain to a five year old what really happened,' says Kathleen. 'Recently, he wanted to know how she had died, so I had to tell him. I'd rather tell him the truth in easy words. We told him that the bold boys weren't allowed into a party and they came back with a gun and although his mammy was shot, it could have been anyone. When Donna died, we told him that his mammy had got broken and the doctor couldn't fix her. We didn't want to say she was sick, because if anybody got sick, he'd think they were going to die. It breaks my heart to have to tell him what happened, but I'd rather him growing up knowing the truth.

'When he's older, we can tell him a bit more. But, to this day, it's very hard for us to talk about what happened. I often go back over that night in my mind and it is very hard. I remember how I came home from a night out with my sisters at about 1.30 a.m. and went to bed. I was only in bed a few minutes when the phone rang. My husband picked up the phone and he just said, "Kathleen, get dressed. Donna has been shot." I couldn't believe what he was saying, but we got dressed and headed straight to the hospital. We were in an awful state, not knowing what was happening, how bad she was.'

The man responsible for shooting Donna was 24-year-old Dwayne Foster, a well-known criminal from Woodbank Avenue in Finglas. On that night in March 2006, Foster and his friends were seen snorting coke and shooting up on heroin, fighting with any-one who got in their way.

Foster was known to the gardaí and they believed he was responsible for a number of ATM robberies, bank heists and drug deals. But, unfortunately, after he was arrested, the unthinkable happened and the Cleary family may now never see anyone brought to justice for taking their beautiful daughter.

According to the *Irish Times*' crime correspondent, Conor Lally, after the shooting, Dwyane Foster and the three people he was with, fled to a house in County Kildare. In total, five people were picked up by the gardaí within 24 hours of Donna's death. Dwyane Foster was taken to Coolock Garda Station for questioning. Foster was a very heavy drug user and when he was in the station, he became unwell and was taken to Beaumont Hospital, which is nearby. The hospital released him quickly and he was sent back to the station. Hours later, he was pronounced dead. It transpired that he was killed by an overdose of methadone that he was taking to stabilise his heroin habit. Because the man who had fired the gun had died, the investigation into Donna's death stalled and the other men who were at the scene with Foster were never charged.

It was a devastating blow for the Cleary family. Gardaí have said that the reason the other three men weren't charged is because they would have to prove, beyond doubt, that the three men knew that Dwyane Foster had a gun and that they were aware that he was going to go back to the house to open fire.

'It's very hard to prove that those three men even knew that Dwyane Foster had a gun,' says Lally. 'So when you can't prove criminal intent on behalf of those three men, unfortunately for the family, the case can't go anywhere.'

The people who actually turned Foster and his gang away from the party weren't aware that Foster was very heavily involved in gangland crime and had come to the attention of the gardaí on a number of occasions over the previous few years. At the time, he had been implicated in a number of armed robberies and was well-known in the area for drug dealing.

Lally says that Donna Cleary wasn't shot because she was in any way involved in gangland crime, she just happened to be at a party targeted by a person who *was* involved in crime. She was the unfortunate victim in all of this.

'The shooting of Donna Cleary goes to prove that when you have a row with a person when you are out at night, you have no idea who you are actually dealing with,' he says. 'You never ask yourself, "Are they involved in crime? Do they have access to weapons or have they taken drugs?" Increasingly, we've seen that even when people are not involved in gangland crime of any sort, they can, at any time, unwittingly come across people who are. They can have rows with them and the people who have access to guns don't have any problem with using those guns to settle even very minor arguments. That's what we've seen in the Donna Cleary killing.'

Days after the shooting, during an irate debate in Leinster House, it emerged that Foster should have been behind bars on the night when he indiscriminately fired at the house on Adare Green, spraying bullets everywhere and killing Donna Cleary. Foster had had a previous conviction. He had lost his appeal and a bench warrant had been issued for his arrest—unfortunately, he was never picked up by the gardaí.

The agony for Donna's family and friends is that, even though three of the men arrested for Donna's murder have spent time in prison for other offences, they may never see anyone serve time for taking her life. Instead, he will now become another statistic on the unsolved crime list.

03 A BRUTAL ASSASSINATION

EDWARD WARD

The night before Edward Ward was shot dead, he had casually asked his wife, Jodie, if she would wear black when he died. It was an unusual question and Jodie remembers being surprised by the conversation, which just seemed to come from nowhere as they lay in bed.

Initially, she had laughed off the question, teasing him by saying that she'd wear white, just to annoy him, but Edward kept talking, 'You know, if I died tomorrow most of those at the funeral would be in black, but only a handful would be wearing it out of love for me.' His young wife, the mother of his two children, thought it was odd that he was thinking this way, given that he was only 24 years old, but she carried on the conversation and had assured him that, of course, she'd wear black, as it was the tradition of the Travelling community of which they were both members.

He had seemed happy with her reassurances and had told her that he loved her before turning over and going to sleep. Jodie remembers lying in bed wondering why in God's name he was thinking of his funeral, but, eventually, she had dozed off.

Friday, 5 October 2007 started off just like any other day in Jodie's mother's home in Clondalkin, Dublin. Jodie, Edward and their children were living with her mother while their house was being built down the country.

The couple had married young and, initially, had set up home in Athenry, County Galway, but Jodie became homesick soon after and moved back to Dublin to be near her family. They got a council house and settled in. Early in their marriage, Edward and Jodie suffered a double heartbreak when their first two baby boys died. Jodie and Edward buried their two baby boys in Esker Cemetery in Lucan, Dublin, but Jodie now plans to have the babies exhumed and laid with their daddy in his final resting place in Tuam.

After the loss of her little boys Jodie gave birth to two beautiful little girls, but Edward was starting to miss his own family in Galway and their trips west became more and more frequent. Jodie started to come round to the idea of the country life and so they both agreed to build their dream home in a small, quiet country village, where their children would be safe—away from the spiralling crime that was ripping its way through Dublin.

It didn't take them long to find a plot of land they liked and they immediately set about designing their new home. For Edward and Jodie, moving into the new house was an exciting prospect, they saw it as a new start for them and their two daughters, Jessica, aged three, and Katie, who was eight months old. The building was going well and Jodie was already buying furniture, curtains and duvets ready to move in as soon as they got the call to say it was finished.

That Friday morning, 5 October, the young couple were busy preparing for Jessica's fourth birthday party, which was being held the following Tuesday. Jodie had most of the plans already made and there were only a few loose ends to tie up before the big day. Edward, who bought and sold vans for a living, was working on some vehicles with his brother, Gerard, and another friend outside. Jodie remembers how he was in his usual good form, and how she was planning for them to go to the cinema that night, or maybe have a meal out. Everything was normal.

'When I look back now, though, I think his death was probably foreshown to him,' she says. 'That morning, he came in and insisted that I take a wad of money from him. I told him that I didn't want any money, that I had money there. And he said, "No get something for the kids and get something for yourself." He told me that if I didn't want to spend it on myself, I should get some more stuff for Jessica's birthday. I told him that I had everything we needed and all that was left for me to do was order the cake. I had her presents and everything sorted. But he insisted that I took the money and even suggested I buy something for my little sister, Sammy Joe, who was only 12. He gave me a kiss and I made him some breakfast and when he was finished he went out the door. I headed off to Liffey Valley shopping centre to order the cake and all of that.'

While Jodie was doing her shopping, Edward rang her from her mother's house to check where she was. 'He was always one for rushing and if he wasn't rushing about himself, he'd be making me rush whatever I was doing. That was the way he was,' she remembers, 'always on the go.'

During the conversation, Jodie told Edward that she would have his dinner ready when he was finished work as she had done the food shopping, but he told her they'd go out for a meal instead. Jodie told him that there was no point spending money in a restaurant when they had food in the house, and that she'd cook their dinner.

When Jodie got back to the house, she did the cooking. Edward's brother, Gerard, joined them along with another pal who had called in to have a chat. Everyone was chatting, mainly about horses, and as the others headed off, Edward came in and told Jodie he was going to Brian Downes's place in Walkinstown. Jodie said that she wanted to go to the movies, but Edward told her that he had to take the log books for some vans as he had to get everything sorted that night.

'I was kind of upset at not being able to go out,' Jodie recalls, 'and I said to him, "Ah, you're all work and no play." As he was going out the door, he asked me to go with him for company. I didn't want to go to be honest but he had this look in his eyes, a sad kind of look, and I thought I might as well go for the drive, keep him happy. He said that when he had his business done, we could head off for a meal or something, even though we'd eaten earlier.'

As the couple drove to Downes's house, they chatted about a trip to New York they were going to take just after Christmas, with their children, and Jodie's mother and sister. They were both looking forward to going away. They also talked about their new house, which was due to be finished in a few weeks, and planned how they would spend their first Christmas there.

'Everything was planned,' says Jodie. 'Edward was really looking forward to the break and he said it'd be a chance to leave all the stress behind and just have a great time. He said the New Year would be great as it would be a new start to everything, with moving into the new house as well. I was so excited about New York. I was looking forward to seeing Edward relax for a change. I used to always say to him, "Why are you always rushing?" He'd always be on the go when he'd be working with the vans. I did a lot of the driving for him, but he just never stopped working. The only day he would take off would be a Sunday, he classed it as a Holy Day and a family day, but for the other six days, he'd be out on the road with the vans.'

Jodie sometimes found it hard to manage everything, as she had to look after the children, the house and drive as well, but Edward would manage to convince her. 'He'd always charm me and I'd fall for it every time. I'd say, "That's it now after this time. I'm not helping you out no more, get someone else." And he'd laugh and say, "But sure you love coming with me, you just deny it but you love coming with me." I'd say back, "Why would I like driving hundred of miles with two kids in the car and with the baby crying?" I would have a go at him, saying he was just looking for a free driver and that I was overworked and underpaid. But I would have done anything for him to be honest. We were so happy together. We went on as if we were still on honeymoon at times. He used to say to me, "You got a good thing when you got me." And I did. I knew I did. He truly loved me and I loved him. And I loved our little drives together, even though I always moaned about them.' Edward had talked many times about their future together. Part of his plan was to work hard enough so that he could retire early and travel the world with Jodie. She used to joke with him that he'd still be planning the trip when he was 80, but Edward worked hard to provide a good life for his family.

———

They had only been married for eight years but throughout their short married life, Edward had always talked about renewing their vows, so he could pledge again his love to his childhood sweetheart. It was something they had agreed to do on their tenth wedding anniversary.

On the evening he was killed, they had decided to take their eldest daughter, Jessica, with them for the drive, but Jodie's mother said she'd look after both the girls. It's something for which Jodie is very grateful. 'Thank God that my mam took them and that Jessica didn't come. I don't know how I would have coped if she had been with us. How she would have coped seeing her daddy murdered.'

They arrived at Downes's garage at roughly 8.45 p.m. Jodie had wanted to wait in the car but Edward insisted that they both go in to the house to say hello to Downes. Downes's mother answered the door and directed them to the yard where her son was working on a car. Downes and Edward started talking and soon they were having a joke and the banter was going back and forth. Jodie was mortified when Edward started joking that he had brought a tall, slim, Polish girl for Downes to 'get together' with, knowing that the joke was at her expense, but she knew what her husband was like, so she just went along with it. Downes started teasing the couple, saying that he was going to go over to New York and sign into the same hotel as them. He said that if they didn't want him to go, then that would make him even more determined to get on a plane. 'We were all laughing and joking,' says Jodie, 'just chatting about different things. We were chatting for ages. It was the longest conversation I'd ever had with Brian, because I usually just left him and Edward at it when they started as they were always messing.'

On previous visits to Downes's, Jodie had stayed in the car when Edward went in to the yard to talk business and discuss the vans—as Jodie found these discussions boring. Edward never stayed long because he knew she was waiting in the car, though she'd sometimes text him to hurry him along.

'Sometimes I wish that I had just sat in the car that night because he would have rushed in and out, knowing I was there, and he'd still be alive today. But it wasn't to be.'

As the three were talking, another man came in to the yard to see Brian, who went over to talk to him. Jodie didn't know who the man was, but she waited with Edward for Downes to finish talking to him so that Edward could conclude his business and they could get on their way. As they were waiting, Edward leaned over and kissed his wife.

When Brian came back, Jodie said that she was going to head out to the car as it was getting cold. She remembers just wanting a bit of heat. Edward started to zip up his coat and told Jodie, as she made her way back to the font of the house where the car was parked, that he'd be out soon. As she waited in the car, she smoked a cigarette and phoned her sister-in-law who had just had a baby.

'I was talking to her for maybe three minutes or so then I hung up and turned on the radio. I'd just got the new Shane Ward CD and I was playing it.'

All the time, Jodie was wondering what was keeping Edward. She thought about beeping the horn to let him know she was waiting but decided against it as she felt she was always rushing him when he visited Downes. So she sat back and waited.

After about five minutes, she saw shadows coming from behind the car and thought that it was the Edward and Downes coming out. She wasn't paying much attention, but then she heard a banging noise, like fireworks, before hearing a loud car or a motorbike drive away.

'But I still didn't pay any attention,' she remembers. 'I keep asking myself, to this day, why did I not look around more? If only

I had looked, I'd have known where it went, but I saw nothing. I noticed people across the road staring over and still I didn't think anything. So when I didn't see Edward coming out I sent him a text saying, "Edward, are you going now?" Maybe half a minute later, Brian's mother comes running out and she was all covered in blood. Because she was old, I thought she had cut herself. She kept telling me to ring the guards but I didn't know what was wrong. I said to her, "Are you OK, love?" She was frantic and she was shouting, "My son's been shot."

Downes's mother was shaking and overwrought and Jodie couldn't really understand, or comprehend, what was being said to her. Downes's mother kept repeating that her son had been shot. As what was being said began to sink in, Jodie jumped out of the car and ran into the house, shouting for Edward, shouting to Edward that Downes had been shot. She carried on running through to the yard, not really looking where she was going.

As she ran, Jodie looked down and saw Edward at her feet. She bent down to see if he was OK. 'I couldn't see any blood on him, but there was blood all over Brian.' As Downes lay dying, gasping for breath in a pool of blood, his young son was standing next to him and watched his daddy die.

———

Brian Downes was blasted a total of seven times with a 9mm Glock pistol. Edward Ward was hit three times with the same weapon by the same hitman who wore dark clothes and a black helmet. The assassin also fired two more bullets which strayed, missing his victims. When he had finished the job, the gunman ran down the driveway and escaped at high speed on the back of a black 1100cc CDS Evolution motorbike.

Gardaí believe Downes was killed for his part in a money-laundering racket. Edward was an innocent witness to the gang-land hit, and that is why his life was taken.

As Downes's young son was trying to help his father, to shake him awake, people were shouting for someone to ring 999. Jodie couldn't see any blood on Edward and one of his eyes was half opened. She was calling his name again and again, but he was still. When she bent down to try to move him, she says she knew he was dead.

People were still shouting to ring 999, but Jodie couldn't press the buttons, she was shaking too much. In the end, she flipped open her phone and pressed to dial the last number she had called—her sister-in-law, Lorraine, in Galway. One of Edward's brothers, Charles, who was visiting his new niece, answered the phone. Jodie was trying to talk through her tears, to tell him that Edward had been shot. When she could make herself understood, Charles said he would contact everyone else. 'I ran back to Edward and, by then, someone else had rung the ambulance and two had arrived, along with the guards. The guard said I couldn't get back in to Edward, even though I begged them to let me see him. They put me into a car and the ambulances headed off to two separate hospitals. The guard kept telling me to calm down and I told her to make sure that they brought me to the right hospital. I told her that the big fellow wasn't my husband, just so that she'd know. She just kept saying, "You'll be OK."'

Jodie was taken to Tallaght Hospital, just 15 minutes away and she waited there for more than 40 minutes for news of Edward.

Jodie was sick with worry and the 40 minutes felt like an eternity. When the doctor came out to see her, he asked if her husband had a tattoo as there was no ID on him. Jodie told him that Edward didn't have a tattoo, the doctor asked her again so that he was certain but she gave him the same answer, her husband didn't have a tattoo. She also said that Edward would have ID on him because he always had it with him. It was then that the doctor told her that there had been a mistake, Edward was at St James's Hospital.

By this time, Jodie's mother had arrived with a friend and all three ran to their car and drove to St James's. Jodie remembers nothing of the drive. She remembers arriving at the hospital and being taken to wait in the family room. She said to her mother that Downes was dead and, even though her mother tried to convince her otherwise, Jodie knew that he was. 'I said to my mother that

they don't come out and ask you about ID unless they're dead—
and then I said, "Edward's dead as well." She said, "No, no. You're
only thinking the worst, everything will be OK." I felt sick.'

Part of the reason Jodie was so worried is that they had been
asked to wait in the family room. After they had been waiting for
about ten minutes, two doctors came in to tell her that, despite
their best efforts, Edward had died.

'I thought I was going to be sick,' remembers Jodie. 'I really felt
myself leave my body, that it wasn't me there, that I was watching
from a distance at this person telling me this had happened. I was
thinking to myself this happens in films, this doesn't happen in
real life, not to good people. And they said it again, but I couldn't
accept it. I kept thinking this couldn't be true. I was hearing it, but
I wasn't listening. They were saying they were sorry and everyone
was smothering me, putting their arms around me and crying and
I'm saying, "No, it can't be true."'

Jodie felt angry at the time—and still does—because she does-
n't know if Edward was alive when he arrived at the hospital and
if she could have been with him for a short while instead of
waiting in Tallaght. But, in her heart, Jodie thinks that Edward was
dead. She says she knew when she knelt next to him in Downes's
yard, but she couldn't accept it.

'I thought maybe they had got it wrong again and maybe it was
Brian Downes who was dead and not Edward. I kept telling them
that I needed to see him, to see for myself that it was Edward, but
they had to take out the tubes that he was attached to before they
would let me go in and they wanted to move him into a private
room. I remember walking into that room and seeing him lying
there, my Edward. I couldn't believe he was dead. I tried to
wake him up, I was shaking him and talking to him, telling him to
wake up, but I knew he was gone, even though he was still warm
to touch.'

After a while, the hospital staff told Jodie that they needed to
clear the room and that everyone would have to leave. By this
time, there were dozens of people gathered at the hospital, crying
in disbelief at what had happened. As his body was now part of a

murder investigation and needed to be preserved, the hospital staff had to stop people coming in to see Edward. Fortunately, his parents and most of his brothers were given permission to say their goodbyes—it would take another week for his body to be finally released back to his family.

Jodie cries every time she talks about the love of her life. They were childhood sweethearts and married in Northern Ireland on Jodie's 16th birthday. They had been too young to marry in the Republic, but neither of them wanted to wait, so the plans were put in place for a ceremony north of the border. Jodie and Edward were second cousins—Jodie's two grandmothers and one of Edward's grandmothers were sisters—something that is not unusual within the Travelling community. The two had known each other most of their lives, meeting up at the usual family gatherings. Jodie remembers how they first got together very well.

'We knew each other for a long time before we went out together. I was visiting relatives in Dublin one time when I was about 13 and he was there, even though he was living in Galway, and he asked me out. I refused first, but he kept on and on at me, so, one day, I thought, Sure what the heck, I'll give it a go. And I went out with him and it progressed from there. When my family moved back to Dublin, he'd come up from Galway to see me. My parents didn't know about it, but he'd come up on the train or whatever and we'd meet a lot of the time in the Liffey Valley Shopping Centre.'

The two continued to meet for the next two years and then Edward asked Jodie to marry him. Although it's not unusual for Travellers to marry young, a lot of people told the couple they were too young. But Jodie says she knew the first time she kissed him that he was the one. They loved each other and so she said yes.

They were married in a small church in Keady, County Armagh, and had their reception at the Holiday Inn in Letterkenny, County Donegal. With almost a year to plan the wedding, the day was everything they wanted. 'I had to get a 'special' dress,' Jodie remembers, 'nothing was good enough for me, so I had to get it made. Everything had to be made. The day couldn't have come quick enough for me. We had a brilliant time and I felt so special. Looking back we were only kids, but we thought we were all grown up. It was definitely the best day of my life and one I'll treasure forever.' Today, Jodie's home is filled with pictures of their wedding day, 29 June 2000.

On every wall, Edward smiles down on his family through the glass of gold-coloured picture frames. He looks happiest in the photographs where he is holding his two little girls, the proud and loving daddy. Jessica is old enough to remember her daddy and talks of him every day. Young Katie, however, was much too young when Edward died to remember how much her father loved her.

Jodie's biggest lament is that her children don't have their daddy near them to share their lives with as they grow older. When she was leaving the hospital the night Edward died, her only thought was how she was going to explain to the two girls, and to Jessica in particular, that their daddy was dead.

'Jessica was so close to him,' she says. 'Edward used to say to me that he loved his children the same, but Jessica came at a time when our lives were so dark and cloudy and she brightened them up, so she had a special place in his heart.'

The young couple had lost their first baby, a boy, when Jodie was 17. He was born a month early, and the couple had no name for him. When Jodie was five months pregnant, doctors had explained that the baby had some problems and they knew that the baby's chances of surviving were slim. The baby lived for only 40 minutes before he died, on 24 August 2001. Jodie and Edward were devastated.

The couple suffered more heartache when their second child, another boy, died when Jodie was seven months pregnant, on 14 March 2002. 'That's why Edward used to always say that Jessica brightened up our lives. We were terrified all the way through the pregnancy in case something went wrong, but thank God she was perfect,' says Jodie. 'And her daddy idolised her.'

Jodie remembers being sick with worry on the way back to her mother's house after Edward had died, wondering how she was going to tell Jessica that her daddy was gone forever. Everyone had told her not to wake the girls that night, to wait until the morning. It had been a horrible night for Jodie, so she went to bed and left her daughters to sleep. All that night, Jodie tossed and turned, crying and thinking how she was going to get through everything without Edward around. How was she going to tell the kids what had happened?

'I obviously dozed off at one stage because when I woke up, I thought, Oh it's a dream, please make all the cars not be outside. That's what I was thinking, if all the cars were not there, it was a dream and I prayed over and over again that it was all just a bad nightmare and I looked out the window and the driveway was filled with cars and I just broke down crying. I knew then it was all very real.'

Jodie now had to break the news to Jessica. At that stage, Jodie hadn't even told her own 12-year-old sister, as she had been in bed when they got home. Jodie knew that the day was going to get worse and worse as it went on.

'I remember when Jessica woke up, she ran in to me and I felt sick. As I cradled my little girl in my arms, I cried and told her that her daddy had gone to Heaven to be with her brothers. I told her that when the sun shines, that's her daddy smiling and when the stars comes out at night time that's her daddy saying, "Goodnight." I said he had to go because he had to take care of the boys and I had to wait here to take care of the girls, because Katie was only little.'

Being a child, the explanation worked for Jessica that day and as everyone was bringing presents for the girls, their attention was on the toys. But things were not so easy the following morning. 'Jessica came in to me crying, and she said, "Mammy, daddy must be crying." I asked her why and she said, "Because the sun isn't out yet, he's not smiling any more." I told her that he was and that she just couldn't see the sun yet, but she said, "No, he's not smiling because he wants to come home. It's not fair, he has to come home." I cried and cried and I tried to explain to her, but it was not good.'

Jessica would listen to her mother's explanations for a short while but then wouldn't want to listen any more. She still talks about her father every day. 'She comes to me and I feel helpless,'

Jodie says. 'She'll cry every night and there's nothing I can do, just be there for her. She says, "I miss my daddy." Or if I shout at her for doing something she shouldn't have done, she'll cry and say, "I want my daddy." If she's with her little cousins and their fathers and mothers are with them, I can see her looking at the daddy playing with his kids and I can see this want in her, as if to say, My daddy can't do that anymore. They say a child can't grieve, but they can. Jessica is grieving, she asks about him every day and misses him and talks about him. She just keeps saying that she wants him back.'

Jessica is a very good child, but Jodie says she has become very withdrawn and gets very angry at times. Edward had bought Jessica a dog last year and she named it Holly, then, after Edward was killed, the dog was run over. All Jodie could think about was how she was going to explain to her eldest daughter that her dog had also died. In the end, Jodie told Jessica that Holly had run back to its mother. When she heard this, Jessica started screaming for her dog and was inconsolable. Jodie told her they could buy a new dog but Jessica didn't want to hear her mother's explanations, saying that she didn't want any other dog because her daddy had bought her Holly.

Jodie feels everything has been thrown on top of Jessica. 'She's too little to understand, yet she understands everything. She listens to everything that's going on. And she's very cute, she's nearly five, but she wouldn't be an ordinary five year old in her mind, she'd be like a ten year old. She remembers everything that went on with Edward and all the memories she had, she talks about all of them.'

Jodie also worries about her youngest daughter, Katie, who will not remember her daddy and the good times they all had before he was killed. 'Jessica has the memories and she has the pain, but poor Katie has nothing. But I know that she'll have the pain of not having those memories. Katie was only eight months old when her father was killed and Jodie is also sad for all the things he has missed too. 'Katie's walking now,' Jodie says. 'With Jessica, Edward was there, but he didn't even get to see Katie's first birthday, her first tooth, nothing.'

Edward didn't get to see Jessica start school the following September either, something both he and Jodie had been looking forward to. When Jodie met the teacher to fill in the usual form for starting school, she wrote 'Rest in Peace' under Edward's name. Jessica has to tell people that her daddy is in Heaven, which is hard for any five year old. 'It's just not fair,' Jodie says. 'He won't see either of his little girls get married. I have to go through all that on my own. I never thought I would be like this, on my own. I wanted us both to live to an old age and see our children grow up with their own children. The people who did this have ruined our lives—ruined our children's lives. And they are still out there on the streets. Still going around as if nothing has happened.' For Jodie, the first Christmas without her husband was horrible. She had to organise all the presents for her children and had to try to be as positive as possible for their sakes. Her mother was her rock, and she knows she probably would not have got through that first Christmas if she had not had her mother at her side to help her cope and stay strong.

'Our first Christmas without him, just weeks after he died, was a nightmare. I will never forget it. All I wanted to do on Christmas morning was cry. The children missed their daddy so much that day. It's a family day and their daddy wasn't there for them. Every Christmas will always be like that now.'

That first Christmas was also a difficult time for Edward's brothers, sisters and parents. They all found it very difficult to cope with such a huge loss.

'The first Christmas after Edward was murdered was the worst of our lives,' remembers Edward's brother, Laurence. 'Most of my family brought the New Year in over his grave. We went to the cemetery that night and, at midnight, we brought the New Year in with Edward and we prayed. I don't think I'll do it again, but I did it that time just because it was our first New Year without him. It was horrible. Some people say the dead can hear, I don't know if they can or not, if they can then he'll know how we feel about him. But Christmas will never be the same again, birthdays will never be the same again, nothing. They say time is a good healer, it probably is, but it won't heal this not until those men are behind bars.'

———

Edward was a larger-than-life figure and everyone loved him. Jodie is aware of what people might think when they hear he was killed in a gangland shooting and it is something she finds very upsetting, because Edward wasn't involved in any kind of crime, he was innocent. She knows that whoever pulled the trigger didn't even know her husband. He just happened to be standing in the yard at the time. Jodie also knows that Edward was unaware of any illegal activities that Downes was involved in. 'I know that for a fact,' she says. 'If he had thought that, he would never have had any dealings with him.'

It was Jodie's own father who had first introduced Edward to Brian Downes, who had been a friend of Jodie's family for years. They were introduced not long after Edward and Jodie had started to date. Downes had been a familiar face in Jodie's house and no one ever had any reason to suspect that he was involved in anything illegal.

'I had known Brian for years and never thought anything bad about him,' says Jodie. 'He was just a character, always telling mad stories that I'd never believe. But he'd have you laughing and that's what Edward really liked about him. When Edward first started selling vans to Brian, he'd see him every few weeks or so, but a few months before he was killed, Brian was ringing all the time, always looking for more vans. Business seemed to have suddenly picked up for him and that was great because it meant more business for us. Edward couldn't keep enough vans coming in for Brian. And Brian would come around to our house and he'd have some food. Just before all this happened, Brian was nearly always here, any-time you'd look around, he was there talking. Never once did I think his friendship with Edward would have resulted in both of them being killed. Edward should be alive now, he did nothing wrong to anyone. He paid his taxes, he lived an honest life. He should be here now with his children.'

She doesn't believe that anyone should be able to take anyone else's life. 'They're not God. They don't give life, so they shouldn't take life,' she says. In her view, anyone who takes a life should be given a life sentence, they should never be allowed out of prison. She knows how precious life is and finds it hard to understand how someone could walk up to another person and kill them and then get on their bike and go, as if they were never there. 'Sometimes when I think back on that night,' she says, 'it's like it was a bad dream, because it happened within seconds of me getting in the car, seeing nothing, knowing nothing. They murdered two men and I was sitting in the car and didn't even know anything.'

Jodie doesn't feel there is any justice for people like her. 'These people can kill and just drive off, disappear into the night and they're gone. They can't be caught. It's not fair. This has to stop. It could be your brother, your sister, your mother, your father, anyone, because it's not just targeted at one person anymore, it's just anyone, it's random. My husband was a good honest person and he was murdered just because he was in the wrong place at the wrong time. It's not even right to say that, because that's not good enough to be saying 'the wrong place at the wrong time' that's no good. He's gone, he won't come back. Edward won't come back and they just disappear into the night and you don't know who they are and why they did it, they're just gone.'

Jodie believes there are people who live around her or within the Travelling community who still believe that Edward had to be involved in something illegal to have been killed that night—and this is in spite of confirmation from the gardaí that Edward had no reason to be killed and had never been involved in criminal activity.

'Edward was through and through an honest person,' she says. 'He wouldn't even take a painkiller because he would tell you it would poison his body. We'd often read stories about drug dealers and he'd say, "The people who take them are bad, but the people who sell them are worse, because they're actually killing people who have a sickness and making huge money from doing it." I know that he wasn't involved in anything bad, but I get looks sometimes where I know people are thinking, Was he, or wasn't he? But he wasn't. I could put my hand on my heart, I could bet my life today that Edward wasn't involved in anything. If he was, it would have come out by now any way. They have nothing on Edward, because there was nothing on Edward.'

But knowing her husband was innocent doesn't help Jodie or her two children. Her one hope now is that someone will realise the devastation that was caused that night, the number of lives that were destroyed and will go to the gardaí. It's her only hope and is something she prays for. She knows she has sympathy from people, but this doesn't help her. 'I would beg anyone who knows anything about that night to come forward. At least if the two men are caught, I could tell my two little girls that the men who killed their daddy were in jail. If there was any kind of justice in this country, Edward wouldn't be dead in the first place, but it might help us all to know who did it. I want to look into their faces say, "Well, it was you who did it!"'

Jodie and Edward were an ordinary young couple. They didn't live their lives looking over their shoulders, worried that someone was after them, they didn't live that way, didn't have that life. Jodie doesn't know if that was how Downes lived.

Jodie is comforted when she goes back to the spot where Edward lost his life. She feels that his spirit is still there. 'I have been to Brian Downes's yard so many times since that day,' she says, 'hoping that Edward would come back, that I'd see him standing there.'

A couple of days after Edward had died, she went to Downes's house to lay flowers and a picture of Edward. The Travelling community is a large one and there were flowers for Edward everywhere. For Jodie, it was too much and she just cried and cried. More recently, now that everything has died down, she still goes there, when she feels up to it, though visiting the yard is always hard. She leaves flowers and tries to remember what happened that night, replaying the events over and over in her head. She imagines Edward sat on the wall, with her laughing at something he has said. But when she stands at the place where she found him, she finds it too much. 'It's just unbearable. I see people staring at me when I'm there, because I'm always crying. Brian's mother has spoken to me since it happened and she said that she ran from Edward to Brian that night, trying to help them. She said Edward wasn't moving, but Brian was still breathing. I knew myself that Edward was dead on the ground, but no one could tell me that that night. No one. They were doing all the work on Brian that night, the ambulance men, but I didn't see them do much with Edward at all.'

Jodie finds it difficult to comprehend that Edward has gone forever. His family take pride and solace in the fact that he was such a large character and he lived every day as if it was his last, always seeing the positive side of life.

'He'd always give out to me over wishing my life away; if it was coming up to our holidays or something. He'd say, "Jodie why are you always wishing time away? For all you know, today could be our last day and you're wishing it away." If we were driving in the car him and I told him I was cold, he'd wind down all the windows. I'd ask him what he was doing as I was so cold. He'd just say, "The sun is shining, it's good to be alive." He appreciated his life and didn't take it for granted. He loved life.'

———

Edward was the 11th of 15 children born to Martin and Nora Ward. He grew up in Tuam, County Galway, alongside his eight brothers and six sisters, in a close-knit family. Edward was always known for being the one who would do a good turn for anyone. As a child, his main love was horses, they were his hobby from an early age. His brother, Laurence, remembers how Edward became an expert at looking after them.

'My father brought us all up with horses. Edward used to go everywhere with him, fairs, marts, the whole lot. He knew a good bit about them and could tell you everything you'd need to know about a horse, their height, their age, just by looking at one. He was a great judge of them. My father reckons that he was probably the best judge out of the whole lot of us, along with my other brother, Bernie. He'd spend all his time when we were growing up taking care of his horses, he loved them and they loved him. His other love was for cars and vans and that's what he got involved in after he was married. We have a pony in Athenry, she's probably 20 years old now, and she's Edward's pony. He has two more, but they're still in Dublin at the minute, they belong to Jessica and Katie.'

When the family were told that Edward had been shot, along with Brian Downes, in a gangland hit, they all knew that Edward had had nothing to do with any gangland crime—and anyone who was associated with Edward knew it too. 'Edward didn't have any secrets, no secret life, or anything like that,' Laurence says. 'When he moved to Dublin he got involved in the motor trade and he got to know a lot of people up there, including Brian Downes. Edward was registered, paid his taxes and all that and everything he did was above board. Brian Downes had some dealership going in Dublin with vans, second-hand vans and cars and that's how he got involved with him. A good few of my brothers knew him actually, but Edward and Brian used to do a bit of dealing every now and then and they knew each other well.

We don't know if Brian Downes was involved in anything, we're not saying he was, but, if he was, Edward knew nothing about it— if he had known, he wouldn't have been there, he wouldn't have been doing any dealing with him. As far as Edward was concerned, Brian Downes was his friend and whatever trouble Brian Downes had with somebody else had nothing got to do with him. Why somebody would come in and shoot Brian Downes and kill an innocent person as well I don't know, but they're just animals.'

Laurence saw his brother on a regular basis and, when they didn't meet face to face, they'd talk on the phone. Everyone who knows the Wards, knows they are a close-knit family and are very proud of their Traveller roots. Most members of the family are living in settled accommodation close to one another. Even when Edward had moved to Dublin, he spoke to his family on the phone most days.

Laurence remembers the last time he met Edward on 3 October, two days before he died. 'We were in Mullingar. There was himself and our brothers, Gerard and Charles, and my friend Brendan McCraven. Edward was in great form and we chatted for about an hour I suppose. He had Jessica with him and wanted me to go for a meal, but Brendan wanted to go home. He was looking very well that night, the best I'd seen him in a long time.'

Laurence left Edward at about 8 p.m. but spoke to him on the phone a few times later that night. On the day Edward was killed, Laurence spoke to him about six or seven times. 'The last time I called, I said, "I want to talk to you for a few minutes, Edward." He said, "I'm with somebody here, I'll ring you back tomorrow." That was the last conversation I had, the last words.'

Edward was with another of his brothers, Gerard, when Laurence called, they had been out looking at horses. Edward had had a problem with a van and was trying to get it going. Laurence came back from the horses at around 9.30 p.m. that night. 'I went upstairs, but left my phone charging downstairs. When I checked later, I had a missed call from my brother, John, so I rang back. I asked him if everything was ok and he said, "Jodie is after ringing, she said that Edward was shot and he's dead." I said, "John, do you know what you're saying?" He just said that he had been told that Edward was gone but he wasn't able to get through to anyone else to confirm it.'

The first person Laurence thought of ringing was Gerard, because he knew that Gerard had been with Edward earlier that evening. But when Laurence got through, Gerard confirmed that Brian Downes had been shot and that Edward had been in the yard with him and had been shot too. 'He then told me that they were in Tallaght and that the doctors are working on Edward, which turned out to be a mistake anyway because the ambulance drivers had got them mixed up. It seems Brian Downes died probably an hour after he was shot, but Edward was killed instantly, he was dead on the ground. He was shot in the back.'

The Ward family had never had news like this before, and never thought something like this could happen to them. 'We had always sympathised with people who had lost their loved ones,' Laurence says, 'but when it comes to your own door and it comes that way, with that news, it's sick. If a person dies good and well of natural causes or if he's killed in an accident, it's hard enough to accept, but when your brother is murdered and he's only in the prime of his life, I just can't explain how I feel and the whole family, we're all just devastated.'

When Laurence had hung up after speaking to Gerard, he headed to Dublin. His wife drove and throughout the journey, Laurence was on the phone as the family contacted one another. The brothers and sisters arrived at the hospital at around the same time. At the time, Gerard and Charles lived in Dublin, and they were already at the hospital with Jodie and her mother when the others arrived.

'All my brothers and sisters made their own way up,' says Laurence. 'Friends, cousins, uncles, aunts, the whole lot went up. But at the time of us leaving, we weren't sure if he was dead or alive. We found out about 30 miles up the road that he was dead, Gerard told me. That's when it sunk in. My mother and father arrived around the same time as myself and my brothers. The doctors wouldn't let me in, they only let my mother and father in to see Edward. In one sense, I know they were trying to preserve all the evidence they had, but they should have let us in. But that's the way it goes, they needed to preserve all their evidence.'

It was a full week before the family got to see Edward again and when they were able to see him, dressed in a suit and laid out in his coffin, he looked like a different person. 'Some people swell up when they die due to the fluids in their body,' says Laurence, 'and that's what happened to Edward. He just looked like a different person. It just didn't look like him to us at all. Even Jessica was saying, "That's not my daddy." She kept saying over and over again, "That's not my daddy. That's not my daddy."'

Even with the reality of seeing Edward in his coffin, the family found it hard to accept that he was actually gone. 'It all seemed so unreal. One night, I'm talking to him and, a week later, you see him dead, and then there's the funeral,' says Laurence. 'What we have gone through, I wouldn't wish on anybody. How somebody can go in there and just kill someone, someone innocent, it's callous, it's cowardly, just blowing a person away for no reason. If they had reason for Brian Downes, they still shouldn't have killed him anyway, they could have done something else to him. But just to shoot an innocent person, I can't understand it, but that's the way it's gone. How many more have been shot since? And will be? The guards are doing their best, but it's up to the Minister for Justice to do something to stop it. They have to form some task force to stop this, they formed the Criminal Assets Bureau (CAB) when Veronica Guerin was murdered. They've got to come up with something else as way to stop all these crimes. There should be no way out for the likes of them. Twenty years is not good enough for them, they should throw away the key—hang them even, hang anybody who does anything like this.'

The Ward family has been torn apart since Edward's murder. Each of them has found it hard to get back to any kind of normality and every day is a struggle. None of them feel they can rest until the person responsible for taking Edward from them is caught, charged and imprisoned.

Edward was well liked by everyone who knew him. His large extended family—his uncles and his cousins—were also friends and they have difficulty not only with the fact that Edward is dead but also with the way he was killed.

'Edward was a bit of a character,' Laurence says. 'He would come down from Dublin, and he'd round up three or four of the lads and go to a pub out the country somewhere and nobody would be able to find him. That's the way he was, he used to go for a few drinks and have a laugh. I'm not a man for drink myself, I don't like it, but I went a few times with him. And I miss him terribly. It's an awful blow. I can't really describe how we feel, any of us. When somebody is just wiped away in a second, words can't describe it. Even if you go out there and you run over a dog, as an accident, you feel very bad about it. How some people can go in there and just shoot people? They don't care about anything.'

Someone from the family visits Edward's grave daily—his father goes every day as does Jodie and some of his brothers—but, although he goes whenever he can, for Laurence, it doesn't help ease the pain. 'I don't think it makes any difference how many times you go to a grave because it's not going to change anything. He's dead, it's a simple as that, it's a fact of life now. The fact that no one has been charged yet goes to show you that they're dangerous criminals that we're dealing with. People have been brought in and questioned.

'They found a motorbike in the canal, they know it was the motorbike involved. Somebody owned that motorbike, somebody knows who was driving it on the night, and whoever was driving it that night shot Edward and Brian Downes. I can't understand it, they find the motorbike and they know there'd be serial numbers on it, probably a chassis number, a registration number and they can link that back to the crime and yet there's nobody arrested for it and charged. They know where the motorbike came from, they know who was involved in it, I'm sure they know who did it, but just to get enough proof on them is the problem. But they will, please God, because we won't let it rest. We want justice for our brother, we want to see them arrested.'

It's important to the family to see somebody charged with Edward's murder—if for no other reason than it will stop them killing someone else.

The family firmly believes that those responsible are from inner-city Dublin, and nothing will distract them from this conviction. Although they know that the gardaí are doing their best, it is frustrating when there still don't seem to be any leads in the case.

The family also believes that the person who pulled the trigger was probably acting on orders and that it's important to get those who made the decisions as well.

'We just want justice for Edward,' says Laurence. 'We want to see these lads arrested. We want to see their faces, we want to see the faces behind the killer, whoever he is, and whoever put the order out on it. It's not only good enough getting the man that shot him and the lad that was driving the bike—they were only doing their job. They were told to go there. Somebody ordered that hit and they have to be got as well and they're the big lads in Dublin, they have to get to them.'

The family's hope is that someone will come forward and tell the guards what they know. Laurence believes the people in the gangs need to realise that they could become targets one day and are in danger of being shot one day too. He hopes this will encourage someone to come forward—so that the men at the top can be stopped.

———

Journalist Conor Lally remembers how 40-year-old Downes had made a name for himself within the criminal fraternity. In his early twenties, Downes earned a lot of his income from buying and selling cars and vans and it was through this trade that he became involved in organised crime. 'He sourced cars and vans for gangland executions and for robberies. He also helped gangs to launder the proceeds of the drug dealing. So while he wasn't on the front line of organised crime, he would have known these gangs very well and worked side by side with them. He had also built up an extensive property empire through the money he got from laundering cash on behalf of gangs. After he was killed, gardaí came to the view that he was probably involved in the drugs trade as well, although his primary activity was supplying vehicles to organised crime gangs.'

It is known that, just before he was killed, Downes had been involved in a couple of property deals and in laundering cash. It seems that some of the deals didn't go too well and some of the people that he had been involved with were members of the gangs causing havoc in a vicious feud in the Crumlin and Drimnagh areas of Dublin. Gardaí believe that he was killed over a deal that had gone wrong.

Not long after Brian Downes and Edward Ward were killed, gardaí knew that Downes had been the target of the shooting.

Edward Ward was not involved in any criminal activity and was simply in the wrong place at the wrong time. He did buy and sell cars and did deal with Downes, but he was not involved in any of Downes's illegal deals.

'Edward Ward was a hard-working man who did his best to pay his way for his young girls and his wife,' says Lally. His killing was particularly harrowing because his wife was sitting outside in the car, and knew nothing of what was happening just yards away. She was lucky in that she had only just gone back into the car minutes beforehand. If she had stayed talking to the men, she would most definitely have been killed too and their two children would have been left without both parents. She is very lucky to be alive today, because the men who carry out these murders would think nothing of shooting a woman at point blank range. Nothing is beyond their remit. This killing came out of the blue completely, but Jodie would have known that her husband was totally innocent. It's very little consolation to her as he is no longer there for her or their children, but she knows that no one can point the finger at her. Edward was an innocent man whose life was ended when it was starting to take off.'

04 THE MURDER OF A YOUNG DAD
JEFFREY HANNAN

W hen Alan Hannan headed off to work at South Hill Community Services on the morning of 22 November 2007, his mind was unsettled. So unsettled that just before 11 a.m., he asked his boss if he could head back home.

He couldn't put his finger on exactly why he was so distracted, why he felt sick to the pit of his stomach, but he knew it had something to do with the fact that his 19-year-old son, Jeffrey, hadn't come home the night before—something that was unusual for the quiet man who's life centred around his family and his little daughter, Nikita.

When Alan had gone into Jeffrey's bedroom that morning to check on him, he had a gut feeling that something was wrong. When Jeffrey didn't phone him to say everything was ok, that feeling grew.

Jeffrey had headed out the night before to get a couple of cans of beer in the local off licence. He had been playing a game on the PlayStation with his young brother who had paused the game whilst Jeffrey went out, so they could start again from where they had left off.

But Jeffrey never made it back home.

The next day his badly beaten and bloodied body was found in a field just yards from his house on Galtee Drive in the O'Malley

Park estate in Limerick, fields where he had played all his life. Gardaí believe Jeffrey was killed with a blunt weapon and, in the days following the attack, they confiscated a number of weapons from the area, bagged and tagged them and sent them off to the Garda Forensic Unit for detailed examinations. The findings of the examinations have not yet been made public and gardaí in Roxboro have to be careful about what information they release as they try to crack this horrific crime. Jeffrey's badly beaten body was callously abandoned in a green area in front of a row of houses where dozens of local children play each day.

Investigating officers believe that Jeffrey's killer had been at a bonfire in the field just opposite Jeffrey's home and that the bright young man had enjoyed his two cans of beer next to the bonfire. At some point, the friendly chat turned into an argument during which Jeffrey was beaten and hacked to death.

The horrific, random killing not only left two parents and a brother and sister in mourning, but also left a two-year-old girl without a daddy, more harrowing was that Jeffrey's former girl-friend was two months pregnant when he was killed. Although the couple were not in a relationship at the time, Jeffrey had played a huge part in Nikita's life and was looking forward to the birth of his second child. He had just enrolled on a barman's training course at a job centre in Limerick city and was hoping to set himself up in a good job.

Alan was very proud of his eldest son, as he is of all his children. He and his wife, Geraldine, had raised their family at their three-bedroomed home in O'Malley Park, an area that had long been associated with drugs and a high level of crime and anti-social behaviour. Alan was one of the lucky dads whose family had never been in trouble with the gardaí. The estate was always in the news and a lot of families in the small estate had lost children to crime. The local graveyard bears witness to the numerous lives lost—especially teenagers and those of young men in their early twenties who somehow became involved in something that was much too big for them and eventually paid the price.

The house where the Hannans lived had originally been the

home of Geraldine's mother and Geraldine had grown up in the cosy little home. She loved being surrounded by the many neighbours and friends they had made over the years and she, and her family, had no intention of ever leaving their home. In their wildest dreams, they never dreamed that the killing of their child would be the reason for their eventual upheaval. Unable to look out of their bedroom window every day and see the spot where Jeffrey had died made it impossible for them to stay.

Alan remembers the cold winter morning they found Jeffrey's body.

'I was actually late going to work that day. Before I headed out, I asked my wife if Jeffrey was home and she said he wasn't. Initially, I didn't think too much of it, but decided that I'd go off and have a look for him in the field where my wife had seen him the night before. I walked all around where there had been a bonfire, because my wife had seen Jeffrey standing there at 1.50 a.m. with another man. She said he had been laughing and was in good form, so she hadn't bothered him. I walked all around the field but saw nothing so I headed back. I didn't see Jeffrey's body which was lying just 20 yards from where I had been standing. Just 20 yards from me, but I hadn't seen him. So I just headed on to work.'

But after he had arrived at work, Alan continued to feel unsettled and worried about his son. 'At 10.50 a.m., a sick feeling came over me and I told my boss that I had to go home. I knew in the pit of my stomach that something was wrong. So I went home and I met Gerard, my wife's brother, going up the hill towards the house. We saw a crowd gathered and the gardaí were everywhere. When I got to the corner someone turned round to me and said there was a body found in the field. And I knew immediately that the sick feeling in my stomach was because that body in the field was my son. I just knew, even before I went over to him. Something had told me that morning to go home, I didn't know what it was but something had just told me.'

Alan went over to the field where Geraldine was standing with their neighbours. She wasn't distraught. The gardaí hadn't let her into the field, so she hadn't seen the body, but, from what the gardaí had said, she knew it was Jeffrey. When Alan arrived, the gardaí asked him to identify the body.

'I can't explain how that feels,' he says. 'Being asked to identify the body of your child. It's just sick to be honest. I just couldn't believe what I was seeing. Walking across the grass that day was my worst nightmare. Every step I took felt surreal, just unbelievable. Seeing my son lying there on the cold ground—dead—I couldn't believe it. He was just slumped on the ground and his face was covered all over in blood. I actually asked the garda if he was dead. I knew he was, but I don't know why I asked. It wasn't as if I had expected him to say, "No, he's still alive", because the people around the area had said that the gardaí had found a body, not that someone had been stabbed or beaten up, but that they had found a body.'

The situation was very hard to accept. Alan says it would have been easier on the family if Jeffrey had been in trouble before or the sort of person who got into fights, but he was the opposite.

After Alan had identified Jeffrey's body, a garda kept asking him if he was ok—but how could he be ok? He was in shock and all he wanted to do was look after the rest of his family. Everyone was devastated—family, friends, neighbours. No one could believe what had happened.

Someone sent for Jeffrey's younger brother, Alan, who had gone to school as normal that morning. They didn't say what had happened or why he was being brought out of school early but, when he got nearer the house and saw the crowd, Alan knew that something was obviously wrong.

It was Alan who had being playing a game on the PlayStation with Jeffrey before Jeffrey had gone out. He had paused the game—it was still on pause the following morning. 'He had been waiting for Jeffrey to come back to finish the game with him,' their father remembers, 'and just happened to fall asleep. To be honest we all still expect him to walk through the door at any moment. None of us can accept that he'll never be home again, that we'll never see him again.' It was two weeks before Alan could accept what had happened to his son. No one in the family could understand why he had been killed, they couldn't take it in.

'I never had any worries about Jeffrey going out at night,' Alan says, 'because he was well liked around the area. He had good friends and he was well able to handle himself. If he was in a scrap with someone, he'd give as good as he got. But I think it took more than one person to do that to Jeffrey.'

At the inquest, state pathologist Marie Cassidy informed the family that Jeffrey had died after receiving a total of ten blows to his head with a blunt object, he had also suffered broken ribs. The cause of death, however, was trauma to the head.

As far as the family is aware, no murder weapon has ever been found. One newspaper had said that Jeffrey had been beheaded with an axe and that a weapon had been found, but that is untrue. Alan remembers reading that article. 'When it came out, we actually wrote to that newspaper seeking an apology, and I got a letter back from the editor saying that under no circumstances was I getting an apology. I was sickened by that. They had printed lies, not even thinking of the family and yet they had no apology. It is very upsetting when you lose a child through murder and the media just write whatever they like, and in this case whatever lies they like.'

Alan also went to the gardaí and asked them if they had given any information to the papers that could explain the story, and he was told that under no circumstances would they give out that sort of information because it would jeopardise the case. Alan doesn't know where the paper got the information that was printed, but it hurt the family a lot—everyone was talking about it. This was one of the reasons that the family decided to have an open coffin for Jeffrey. 'We decided to let people see Jeffrey before we buried him,' says Alan, 'but it didn't look like him at all. He had a look of fear on his face that was indescribable. Every photograph that we ever took of Jeffrey, all the photos in the house, show him smiling. He just always had a smile on his face. But to look in that coffin that night and see him lying there, that wasn't the Jeffrey we knew. The look of fear on his face was terrible. And he had a number of stitches where his face had been repaired. My wife has constant nightmares about it. All of my family said it wasn't the

Jeffrey they knew lying there, because we knew him as a jolly person. He looked awful.'

Both Alan and Geraldine are finding it very hard to move on with their lives since their son died. It is as if time has stood still.

'From the day we found him lying in that field, it has been like living a nightmare,' Alan says. 'It really was hell right from the beginning. But I busied myself by organising everything for his funeral. There were people coming in and out all the time, sympathising. The house was always busy. But it's really after the funeral that it all hits you. You're suddenly on your own. People feel that if they come knocking at the door they're imposing. But what they don't realise is that this is when things get worse—when you are on your own and have time to think. You end up sitting at home looking back on the day and asking yourself, "What if?" What if we had done this? What if we had done that? Could we have prevented him from going down the road that night? If Geraldine had called out to him from the top window at 1.50 a.m. would he still be alive? It's all ifs and buts.'

Alan was out of work for three weeks after Jeffrey died. His employer was very good to him and gave him the time off he needed to help him get over his son's death but the worst thing for Alan was to sit at home. 'You could drive yourself crazy thinking about things constantly. You're better off getting out there, keeping active and doing something to keep your mind occupied.'

Something that does occupy Alan's mind daily is the rumours of who killed his son. On the morning that Jeffrey's body was found, people started to talk. A couple of names were mentioned to him, names of people he knew who were believed to be responsible for the murder. Alan would see the people mentioned on the street every day and it devastates him to think they could have beaten up Jeffrey, could have killed his son, and that he doesn't know for certain. He still sees them and wonders if it was them, but he can do nothing, even if they know what they did. Alan knows he has to leave the investigation to the guards. But he finds it hard. His son's death is at the back of his mind all the time, but he knows he has to trust the gardaí, trust them to do their jobs and make sure that those responsible are caught and made to pay the price.

The guards contact him every couple of weeks. There have been a lot of things happening in Limerick and Alan thinks they are inundated with information about different events. There have been at least five murders in the area since Jeffrey died and there is one garda station investigating them all. 'They're doing what they can in relation to Jeffrey,' Alan says, 'but I know it's going to be hard, and we just have to wait and hope that there will be a conviction.'

Having Jeffrey's children around has been a great help to the family, helping them to move on but, at times, it's also very difficult as they have to try to explain to a little girl, almost on a daily basis, that her daddy has gone for ever.

'Nikita gets up every morning and she looks straight up at the picture behind me and she wants to kiss her daddy,' Alan says. 'She actually says, "Daddy, kiss." Every morning when she gets up, she remembers him. She's a clever little kid. Through social workers, we also have custody now of Tianna, Jeffrey's second little girl. She's five months old now. Their mammy isn't well and we are taking care of both of them full-time. I have to admit that it is hard bringing up the children at our age, but we love them so much that it doesn't bother us at all. Geraldine looks after them in the mornings when I go to work. I come home at around 5 p.m. and I take over then. I'll have them then till the following morning and we'll switch again. But we take turns looking after them, they're great kids and all we have left of Jeffrey now.'

They take the children with them everywhere. Alan has noticed that when they go into town to the shops, people pass them on the street and stare at them all—it is something that he gets uptight about. He feels that if people said something to him, something like, "Sorry about your son", then you'd accept it, but when people stare at his face and say nothing, Alan finds it hard to take.

He knows people may try to understand but when he is asked, "How're you keeping now?", all he can think is unless it has happened to you, you'll never know. He admits that it is something he has actually said to people. 'I met a woman in South Hill whose husband was murdered as well, and I'm glad that I met her because we could actually sit down and talk. She was a stranger to me at the time but I could sit down now and talk to her about things that I couldn't talk to a normal person about, a person who hadn't the experience of losing a loved one. People who haven't lost a child just don't understand what we are all going through. It's a total nightmare. And we are going through it every single day of the week. Every morning when I get up, I realise that my son isn't here. It's very different losing a child in this way, completely different to losing a child in an accident. This was a callous murder. And unless your child has been murdered, you can never know what it's like to get through each day.'

One of Jeffrey's best friends, Richard 'Happy' Kelly, went missing in April 2006. Two years later, his body was found in a lake in County Clare. He had been murdered before his body was dumped in the lake. His mother is campaigning for justice for her son. She is not alone. Jeffrey's dad talks about another woman, who he met through his community work, whose son has been missing for ten years. The woman is in her seventies and all she wants is to get her son back so that she can bury him. She has told Alan that she would die happy if she could get her son's body back and give him a proper burial. 'Up at the graveyard,' Alan says, 'just in the area where Jeffrey is buried, there are at least 12 young people under 20 years of age who have been murdered, or died because of drug abuse. I used to go to the graveyard years ago to visit my grandmother's grave and, back then, it was all people over 40 who were being buried, but you go there today and all you can see are headstones for young people.'

· Alan thinks the problems today, the reason so many young people are being killed, are because where he lives has changed—mainly because of the availability of drugs. 'When I was growing up, we didn't even know what a drug was, we just went out and enjoyed ourselves with our pals. I joined the army when I was 17 and when I turned 18, I had my first drink with my father. I had a pint of Guinness. There was no drug taking back then and if you had a fight with someone, you went out fist to fist, back into the pub afterwards and shook hands and had a drink with him and that was the end of it. But you can't have a fair fight any more. It's all guns, knives and whatever. With the way this society is today, you'd be frightened to bring your kids up.'

Even with all the heartbreak his family has been through, Alan still feels that there is some hope for the area in which he lives and that there will be more opportunities for the younger children growing up there today. 'I'm optimistic about the future of Limerick, because with the regeneration work going on at the moment, they're taking down areas like South Hill and building them up again as good housing estates—they will probably vet the people going in there to see if they have been involved in any trouble or anything like that before they allocate them a house.'

Even with his optimism, Alan knows it won't be easy. 'At the moment in areas like South Hill and Weston, there are kids of about 12 or 13 who are little gurriers, running the areas for the bigger boys. The bigger ones tell them what to do—"Break that window" or "Drop off this or that"—and these kids think they are big, getting a name for themselves, so they will do whatever is asked of them. These kids crave power. They have this attitude whereby they send out the message that they are involved in a certain gang and no one can touch them. And they are going around making a lot of money out of what they are doing. So although they are trying to change the look of the area, I worry for the future of those kids.'

For Alan, education is one of the things that can make a difference. Most of the young 'gurriers' play truant and don't stay in school and he thinks a way needs to be found to keep them there, away from the control of the main criminals in Limerick.

'I reared my kids the way I was brought up myself and my father was very strict. If you did something wrong, you got a clatter for it. You wouldn't do it again. So I put the same thing into my family, it's the way I knew and my kids turned out grand. I know I was probably one of the lucky ones, but I never had any problems with them growing up. When I asked them to do something, they did it. When they went out, they knew that they has to be home at a certain time and even when our daughter Emily was 18, she knew that she had to be in by 10 p.m. because I wouldn't have it any other way, especially in an area like South Hill where you couldn't be certain about what might happen. Although I never thought I would be going through this now, having to cope with the murder of one of my children.'

Alan and Geraldine's three children—Jeffrey, Emily and young Alan—were all aware of what was going on around them, with the crime and drugs in the area, but, to their parents' great relief, none of them showed any interest in that way of life. Alan believes that people should be allowed to live their lives—earn a living and raise their children—without being harassed by others. As he says, 'If you don't bother people, they shouldn't bother you.' But he knows life isn't that easy, or simple, and that there are people who want to control those around them and have power over them. It is a situation that he finds hard to accept and it angers him on a daily basis.

'I don't think anyone could understand the anger that I'm going through at the moment about what happened to Jeffrey. I don't know how I'm still walking around to tell you the truth, I'm not showing any emotion or anything, but it's there inside me, a lump in my throat that I just can't get rid of. I actually took relaxing tablets after it happened and sleeping tablets, but they didn't do anything for me. It's terrible to say this but I could be having a conversation with someone and they could be talking to me about something really important but I wouldn't even be listening. He is such a big loss to all of us.'

Counselling is not something that many men agree to lightly, but it can be a great help when dealing with something as incomprehensible and devastating as murder. Through counselling, many people can find a way to move on with their lives. But it doesn't always help—something that Alan learned very quickly. 'I went to counselling once and I actually sat down with a lady counsellor and she was asking me what happened and how I felt. But I found that it only made me worse, talking to a stranger who didn't really understand what I was going through. I'd prefer to talk to my own family about it. My wife, my kids and myself sit down now and we talk, we actually talk about it and it helps in some way. But it's a living nightmare, it's unbelievable.'

The Hannon family was very close. Alan's pride and love for his murdered son are obvious in the way he speaks of him. 'He was a great kid. As he grew up, we went to the hurling matches together and we'd have a drink and he'd have the craic. He was very jolly, he was always smiling, nothing ever fazed him, he was an easy-going kind of young fella. When his first daughter was born, he actually stayed in the hospital for three days, he wouldn't leave. He had no food, nothing, but he didn't mind, he was so excited about Nikita being born, he adored her.'

After Nikita was born, Jeffrey's young family moved in with Alan and Geraldine, who helped to look after the baby. Not long after though, Jeffrey and his girlfriend started to argue and Jeffrey moved to England for a fresh start. He left his young daughter with his parents to give her some stability whilst he tried to settle himself. His girlfriend followed him over but things still didn't work out and Jeffrey moved back to his parents' house. 'And he was here five weeks when he was murdered, just five weeks,' Alan says in disbelief.

Alan knows how good Jeffrey was to his daughter and how he was eager to better himself so that he could give her a better life.

'He loved Nikita so much. He'd get up during the night and make her bottles. He was a great dad. I still cannot believe that he isn't here and that he'll never see his children grow up.'

Jeffrey was well liked by everyone who knew him. Alan remembers his son as someone who had so much to offer in life. 'He was really good with his hands and he was always doing something, fixing up a bike or cleaning windows for people. He loved to keep busy. When he was growing up, he'd clean gardens for the neighbours, or go to the shops for them, and he'd get a few bob for doing it. When he was in his late teens, I remember one neighbour telling him that he was getting too big to give money to when he was doing a favour for her, so she'd give him a couple of fags instead and he was delighted with that.'

Jeffrey had just finished his Leaving Certificate with the Limerick Youth Service and was hoping to get a good job. His family were optimistic too because his attitude was so positive. He'd always make the effort and go out and do things rather than sitting around.

Alan still finds it difficult to keep going, to get up in the morning and go to work because he is thinking of Jeffrey all the time. During his lunch hour, he goes straight to the graveyard from work, he rarely gets anything to eat. 'The only way I have of believing that he is gone is by looking at the headstone and seeing it right there in front of my eyes, seeing his name on a headstone. I actually picked it out myself and had it erected after a couple of weeks, just to make sure that there was something there that we could go up to and look at. I didn't want us going up to look at a hole covered in with soil. The graveyard is a place where I can go to clear my mind and sit down and have a chat with Jeffrey. I can actually go up there sit down and talk to him.

'My dad is up there as well and I go to his grave and I always ask him to look after Jeffrey. I remember on the day of the funeral, there was thunder and lightning, and my brother was walking behind me as we followed the hearse going up to the graveyard. The first thing he said was, "There's Dad looking after Jeffrey." Every time I go to the graveyard now that sticks in my head, and I just hope and pray that that is the case.'

Alan often wishes that he could turn back time and relive that fateful night, so that things could be different, so that he would still have his eldest son around him. He often thinks, If only Jeffrey had stayed in England or If only we had told him not to go out that night. 'When he asked Geraldine for the two euro for the couple of cans, I was going to say to him that I had a few bob upstairs and we could go down to the pub for a couple of pints. But because I had work the next day, I didn't say anything. I often think back and wonder about why I didn't say it. Something stopped me and I don't know why.'

Alan knows it's easy to become distracted and caught up in the 'what ifs', the things that might have been. He knows that he and his family have to find a way to accept what happened and to carry on living their lives, even though their hearts are broken.

For Alan and his family, one of the hardest things to come to terms with is the randomness of Jeffrey's murder. They can't understand why he was killed. 'If Jeffrey, had been involved in crime or gangs or drugs or anything like that, I could accept something like this,' Alan says. 'You'd know something like that was going to happen eventually—the way things are going today. But Jeffrey wasn't involved in any sort of crime or anything like that, so I never expected it. That was the last thing I could have imagined that morning, that I would have to identify the body of my dead son.'

Alan still goes over the events of the day Jeffrey died as if it was yesterday, they are absolutely clear in his mind. 'For six weeks after we found him, I couldn't eat. Not a thing. My stomach started to close and I couldn't hold down any food and I lost a lot of weight. I went down to about seven stone. I got a couple of things off the doctor, food supplements on prescription, and it helped build me back up a small bit. It hit me very hard. Nothing is the same for us. I went to a hurling match recently and I just couldn't get into it. It just wasn't the same without my son. It was the same when I went to the All-Ireland final, my heart just wasn't in it at all.'

———

Jeffrey's murder had a huge impact on everyone in the Hannan household. Emily and Alan Junior have been terribly affected by what has happened. Emily was very close to her brother and they often talked through problems that either of them might be facing, the small worries in life that everyone has to deal with.

In many ways, Emily and Jeffrey were more like best friends than brother and sister. Emily knew that Jeffrey's break-up with his girlfriend had taken its toll and that Jeffrey had been feeling depressed since he came back from Manchester. He had spent a lot of time in the house in the five weeks he was back and had asked his mother to sort out his medical card. He wanted to go to the doctor to get something to help him relax. Throughout this time, Emily had tried to reassure him that everything would be OK. She remembers that his biggest worry was for his little girl. The morning after Jeffrey had been killed, when her father called her on her mobile, Emily's first thought was that her brother had tried to hurt himself in some way.

'I was three months pregnant,' she remembers, 'and I was living with my partner in his mam's house. I thought something had happened to Jeffrey because of the break-up with his girl. I thought he must have done something silly and I wasn't expecting to hear that he had been murdered. I thought it was something stupid. When my dad rang, he said, "Emily, it's Jeffrey. You need to come home, it's Jeffrey." I told him I'd be up in a minute because I didn't think anything of it at the time. I got a taxi up the road and I saw that all of O'Malley Park, where our house is, was cordoned off with white tape. But I still didn't think anything bad had happened to Jeffrey. I didn't think it was anything to do with him. But when I got out of the taxi, I got this sensation over me, it was like some kind of hot feeling in my stomach. My partner was with me and he was saying that Jeffrey had probably cut his wrists or something over his girlfriend, over him not being with her and all. But when I got to my mam's door, there were people coming in and out of her house. Then I looked over across the green and there was a white cover over in the green covering the area.

'Before I even got into the house, people were looking at me oddly—all the neighbours—and my mam was sitting on a chair. I could see that she was in shock and I asked her what was wrong. I asked her if it was Jeffrey and she just said, "Yeah." She said no more. I went upstairs because I thought he was up there. As I walked around the house, I kept saying, "Where's my brother? Where's my brother?" Then one of my mother's neighbours followed me and said, "You need to sit down, because you're pregnant. I have to tell you something." I told her I wanted to know where my brother was and she said, "Emily, you have to listen to me. You have to sit down." Then she said, "Your brother is dead.

Your brother is dead." I just stood there in shock. I kept asking her how he could be dead. Why was he dead?

'I remember asking her if he had killed himself. I couldn't believe what I was hearing when she said he had been murdered. I just felt sick. It was a nightmare. We were all in bits. We just couldn't take it in. We kept asking why. There was no reason for anyone to kill Jeffrey because he never asked for trouble. He was never in any trouble.

'Over the next few days, people in the area started to talk and we heard all sorts of stories, like he was murdered because he had been fighting with someone and they had mentioned something about his girlfriend. Then we heard he'd had a fight over football, but Jeffrey knew nothing about football. He only followed Manchester United because my boyfriend, David, followed them, he never even knew when they were playing unless David said something to him.'

Emily believes that there is a cover-up in O'Malley Park, and it angers her. She is convinced that a lot of people know exactly what happened that night—and exactly who killed her brother. 'I know that certain people in O'Malley Park know who killed Jeffrey because people talk. And it makes me wonder who can be trusted. I often walk past certain people and think to myself, Oh God, was it them?, but you can't point fingers at people when you don't know for sure. Sometimes, I feel like I can't trust anyone. I feel numb. I don't know if my friends are my friends. I wonder about everyone. I hate it when people talk about me behind my back and I often see it. Someone will walk past me and as soon as I'm gone, they'll say, "That's Jeffrey Hannan's sister, the fella who was murdered", and that really upsets me. Sometimes they don't even realise that I have heard them and they are staring at me behind my back.

'A lot of people in the area are afraid to say what they know because they just want a quiet life. Jeffrey's murder really shocked people up there because they know what he was like, how quiet he was. I think that's why it's harder for us to accept that he died like that. Fighting was not in Jeffrey's nature.'

Emily misses having her big brother around to talk to. She gets upset about the fact that he will not be around to see his niece grow up, and that her daughter will never know her uncle. She remembers how much Jeffrey was looking forward to the birth of her child, who she named Abby. When Abby is older, Emily says she will tell her about her uncle, what kind of person he was, and she will also tell her about how he died.

Emily is also saddened by the affect Jeffrey's murder has had on her family. She feels they have become bitter and that they don't talk to one another the way they used to. She thinks her family has changed a lot, that everyone is different and she knows it isn't fair. They are all trying to move on, but life isn't the same for any of them any more. There was a lot of support for the family at the time of the funeral but when it was over, life moved on for those around them and the Hannan family was left to cope.

'Just waking up in the morning, knowing your brother is not here, is very hard, especially when we were so close. On the 22nd of every month, I always think, Oh God, it's another month. Sometimes, it feels as if it's a dream and I'm going to wake up and it will all be OK. But of course it never is OK. If I could look into the eyes of whoever murdered my brother, I would ask them why. Why did they kill him? They took away an innocent person who now has two children, one he never even had a chance to see. For what reason? There could have been no reason to kill Jeffrey. It's as simple as that. All we have left now are memories.'

Emily feels lucky because she got on so well with her brother. As kids, they had had the normal arguments—she remembers that he used to run away with her pram—but they had got beyond that. They become closer after Emily left home to move in with her boyfriend, when they were no longer under each other's feet. Jeffrey would call up to see Emily and her boyfriend and would watch the football with them. They would have a chat and a few cans and enjoyed the craic.

Jeffrey's murder has also changed the way Emily views the area she grew up in. She is nervous walking around and feels paranoid. It's a fear that will probably live with her for the rest of her life. 'I'm looking behind me the whole time. A fear is always there now, that I never had before. A fear that they could do this again. To any of us. When I lived up there we knew it was bad, there were burned out cars most nights and a lot of drug dealing, but you just had to stay out of trouble. It was probably very hard for some people to say no to drugs because they keep trying to push them on you, but we never got involved because my dad made sure. He was strict with us and we did what he said.'

Jeffrey's younger brother, Alan, is also finding it hard to cope. Their father remembers that the two brothers had a good relationship, even if they were always arguing about the PlayStation and who was going on it next. Now, Alan is heartbroken. He goes to St Enda's School and had always been a good student but, his father feels that Alan's personality has changed since Jeffrey's murder. 'Alan took his death very badly. He has started to snap at teachers and he gets into trouble now, something that never happened before. He was always a good kid, always getting good school reports. I think he is finding it very hard to accept that his brother is dead.'

Alan is seeing a counsellor in school and he is starting to come to terms with what happened but his family have found it very difficult to watch him. 'It's heartbreaking for us looking at him because we can do nothing to make things better,' Alan Senior says. All he wants is to have his big brother back. And we can't bring him back. Alan was very like Jeffrey in that he was a quiet lad. Now, he comes home from school and he goes up to his room and you wouldn't see him until he is hungry. He just keeps himself to himself. He has just distanced himself from everyone. He goes to his room and he plays with his PlayStation. It helps to take his mind off things.

'Before Jeffrey died, Alan had asked me to get him a PlayStation 3 but I didn't have the money at the time so he asked me to get it for his birthday. I told him that I wouldn't have the money, but that I'd give him a few bob anyway. But when Jeffrey was murdered, the first thing I had to do for Alan was to go out and buy him a PlayStation 3. No matter what happened, I knew that I'd have to get him the one thing that would take his mind off what was happening. He loves soccer and hurling, too, so he watches a lot of sport on TV and his love for sport is one of the things keeping him going because he can get out and play a game of football or hurling and it keeps his mind off things.'

The Hannons left O'Malley Park the January after Jeffrey died, because they couldn't bear the thought of coming out of their front door and seeing he place where Jeffrey had died across the way. Every time Geraldine looked out the window where she last saw Jeffrey, it brought tears to her eyes and the family knew she couldn't go on like that. Geraldine didn't want to move but she was left with no choice. She had lived there from the day she was born. The family can remember what the area used to be like and about how much it has changed. 'It has a lot of bad memories for us now and I hate going up there,' says Emily. 'I moved out when I became pregnant because it had gone so bad. I didn't want to rear a child there. And yet I never thought things had gone that bad, bad enough for my brother to be murdered just a few feet from where he lived. The area gets a very bad name, but there are a lot of really good people up there and the support we got when all of this happened was unbelievable. '

The Hannons know people made assumptions about Jeffrey when they heard he was murdered in O'Malley Park, because it has such a bad reputation for crime and drugs, but the family knows it has had nothing to be ashamed of. 'We have good kids,' says Alan, 'and there was no reason for us to be embarrassed. Then you have some of the newspapers printing things about Jeffrey claiming that he was involved in gangland crime and that hurt, because he was just an innocent 19-year-old, never involved in trouble, but when you see that written it just makes you sick. But we have to forget about that and move on.

'Jeffrey was an innocent victim. He was in the wrong place at the wrong time, that's what we believe. That night was his first time to go out, after five weeks back in the country. And to think that he was murdered just yards from his hall door. He was the type of kid who wouldn't hurt a fly. But I believe that whoever did that to Jeffrey must have been out of their heads that night on drugs because what they did was simple savagery. We had rung my daughter, Emily, and my sister at about 11.30 p.m. because we started getting worried about him. The last thing I thought that night was that he wouldn't come home ever again.'

———

Jeffrey's father knows it would help his family if someone was convicted for Jeffrey's murder. He finds it difficult to think of the person, or people, who killed his son, to think of them alive when Jeffrey is dead. But, equally, even if people were convicted, he finds it hard that their parents and friends could still visit them in prison and talk to them, when he can never see Jeffrey again and never sit and talk to him.

'All we want now is justice for Jeffrey,' says Alan. 'We would like to see the person, or people, who did this put behind bars because I don't think anyone should get away with murder these days. No one has the right to take a life.'

'The one wish we all have is to have things as they were before, with Jeffrey back with us. But we know that's impossible. So for Jeffrey's sake we just pray that he can rest in peace and the person responsible for killing him gets what he deserves.'

Alan says that if there was one thing he could say to the people responsible for his son's death, it would be to urge them, beg them, to go to the gardaí and confess. He finds it hard to believe that they can wake up every day and not think of the damage they have done to so many people by murdering such a young and innocent man. 'We are living a nightmare so surely what they have done is eating them away. If it's not, then they don't have a conscience. They know they have done wrong and they are going to be caught for it one way or another. The gardaí have promised me that there will be a conviction. It's just a matter of time. So they are better off handing themselves in. If there are people out there, and we know there are, who know the people who did this, then they should just make an anonymous phone call to the gardaí and tell them what they know. I know the gardaí have to be 110 per cent certain of the evidence they have because they don't want these people to walk free, so we just have to wait.

'Being honest, if they did walk, I'd probably end up in prison myself because I would do something that I shouldn't do. That's the way I feel at the moment, it's the anger inside me. I don't care about anything anymore. Taking revenge would be against everything I have ever stood for, but the way I look at it is this—if I was in Jeffrey's position and it was me who was in the ground and Jeffrey was here in my place, he'd be above in Limerick Prison. We were a close-knit family, we always looked after one another. And I know that he would not let anyone get away with murdering his father and I owe it to my son not to let his murderers get away with taking his life. That's the way I feel at the moment. I know the anger I have inside me is probably unnatural, but my life has been destroyed.

'Nobody can imagine how our lives have been turned upside down. When Alan goes out in the evenings, if he goes over playing his hurling match or anything, we worry sick about him until he comes back in through the door. Even when he's at school, his mother waits around for him, and if he doesn't come in by the time we give him, she goes crazy with worry. She phones me at work straight away. There were a couple of times when I went out looking for him and he was actually at football training in the school, but he forgot to tell us. We're now over anxious and we wouldn't have been like that before Jeffrey's death. We always trusted our kids, they went out and did whatever they had to do and came home. But since this happened to Jeffrey, we're conscious of things happening around the place all the time.

'That day changed everything in our lives, every single thing. We had a great outlook on life for the kids. But now we just try and get through each day. We have no plans for the future because to us the future means nothing right now. We haven't planned a holiday, we don't organise to go places, we just get up and get on with the day and go to bed at night. We buried our son and all we have left of him now are his children. It's a big comfort rearing

Nikita. At least we can look at her proudly every day and see her daddy. We want what's best for her now. It's our job to make sure she is OK. We dread the day when we will have to tell Nikita and Tianna what happened to their daddy. Nikita knows that he's not here. I bring her up to the graveyard and before she gets in the gates, she'll actually calls out, "Daddy." She knows that he's in there. Even going up the hill where Jeffrey was found she calls out for her daddy, it's very odd. I think it will affect her very badly when she gets older—and her little sister, too, who never even knew her father.'

———

Billie Barrett is a youth worker at the Limerick Youth Centre in South Hill. He knew Jeffrey very well and had worked with him on various courses over the years. The last time he spoke to Jeffrey was the night before he was killed. When he learned that Jeffrey was dead, he was shocked to hear the cheerful lad he knew had been murdered so brutally.

'I was parked up outside the job centre in South Hill the night before, and I saw Jeffrey jogging across the road towards me. I hadn't seen him for a while and I asked him when he had got back from England. It was great to see him and he was beaming, in great form. He told me that he was starting a course as a barman and he was laughing saying that he'd be delighted with himself behind the bar drinking all the profits.

'It was great to see him in such good humour. He was always a happy fella, always seemed to be smiling and he had loads of friends in the courses. When one of the lads came in that day and said that Jeffrey had been murdered, I was in shock. I just wasn't the better of it. We were all devastated. He was such a lovely lad and I was sick that I had only been chatting to him the night before and he was in such good form. I just hope that they get whoever did it soon, for the sake of his family.'

Some of Jeffrey's friends, heartbroken when they heard of his death, wrote a poem in his memory. The poem sums up how they felt about him as a friend. They dedicated it to 'Twiggy', Jeffrey's nickname.

> For the young man we loved so dearly
> And the man he was meant to be
> He will never really know now just how much he meant to me
> So may the wind carry you home to your final resting place
> And always in our dreams may we see your smiling face.

To date, six people have been arrested in relation to Jeffrey's murder and all have been released without charge. Alan Hannan does sometimes worry that Jeffrey's case will never be solved.

'Every time someone gets killed in Limerick, Jeffrey's case is put on the back boiler And there's nearly a murder every day, so God only knows when we'll have an end to all this. But whoever did that to Jeffrey could do it again to someone else so they have to be brought to justice.'

Alan placed a special plaque on Jeffrey's grave just weeks after his death. It holds his heartbreaking message to his child: 'Any man can be a son, but it takes someone special to also be a friend.'

'He was my first son,' says Alan. 'He was my friend and my pride and joy. And I will not be happy until I meet up with him in Heaven.'

The city of Limerick now has the highest murder rate in Europe.

05 | **BURNED TO DEATH**
EMER O'LOUGHLIN

On the morning of Friday, 8 March 2005, Josephine O'Loughlin, a mother of four, was sitting in her home in Dublin watching television as Pope John Paul ɪɪ was laid to rest at St Peter's Basilica in Rome.

What Josephine could never have known was that as she, and millions worldwide, were mourning the death of one of the most popular papal leaders in history, her youngest daughter, Emer, was burning to death in a blazing caravan in a remote field in County Clare.

Emer O'Loughlin, a pretty 23-year-old brunette, was a student at the Galway Mayo Institute of Technology and a budding artist. She should have been in college on the day she was murdered, but the campus had closed as a mark of respect to the late pope. As a result, Emer was alone in the mobile home she shared with her long-term boyfriend, Shane Bowe.

The couple had set up home on the site in Ballybornagh, between Kinvara and Tubber—an area known locally as Newline—which was owned by Shane's mother. She had thought it a handy place for them to live and that living there would save them the expense of paying rent for a house.

However, Emer and Shane weren't the only ones living in the

area. A short distance away in an adjoining field, another man lived in a caravan on his own. It was in this man's caravan that the promising young artist met her death.

That March morning, when the fire service and gardaí arrived to battle the blazing caravan, they did not know that Emer was trapped inside, in a fire which had covered the surrounding fields in thick black smoke. But as the flames died out, leaving nothing but smouldering ashes and a blackened carcass of steel, officers started to pick their way through the glowing embers and stumbled across a burned out human carcass.

Within minutes, the area was cordoned off and a full-scale investigation was started.

Because of the horrific condition of the body, the deputy state pathologist was unable to officially confirm the gender of the victim when he first arrived at the crime scene. However, extensive DNA tests carried out by the Forensic Science Laboratory at Garda Headquarters in Dublin subsequently confirmed that the body was that of Emer O'Loughlin.

An initial post mortem, conducted at University College Hospital in Galway, failed to establish the exact cause of her death and could not rule out sexual assault. Therefore further forensic and technical examinations were ordered.

An Indian Kukri knife, of the sort used by the Gurkhas in Nepal, was also found at the scene. The distinctly shaped weapon, one of the most lethal knives in the world, is made of thick heavy steel with a blade so sharp that it is used mostly for wood cutting. Nobody knows if this weapon was used by Emer's attacker before the caravan was set ablaze as her body was so badly burned by the raging fire.

The killing baffled gardaí. They couldn't understand why someone would want to murder and then burn this quiet young woman. They also didn't know where the owner of the caravan was.

In his appeal to the public, Superintendent Paul Mockler, who was leading the investigation, stated that at around 7.30 a.m. on the morning Emer was killed, a car with a loud engine was seen leaving the mobile home site at Ballybornagh, travelling in the direction of Gort. He appealed for the driver of that car to come forward—but to no avail.

Two days after the murder, the main suspect in the case, barricaded himself inside a stone fort at Dún Aengus on the Aran island of Inis Mór. Tourists who witnessed the man making repeated threats to jump off the 300-foot cliff, immediately notified the gardaí.

Following a harrowing four and a half hour ordeal, officers managed to overpower the agitated man. They brought him to St Brigid's Psychiatric Hospital in Ballinasloe where he was examined and admitted as a patient. However, he was released five days later.

On 18 April, three days after he left the hospital and ten days after Emer's murder, the man emerged once again on the clifftop at Dún Aengus. When gardaí arrived, they found a bundle of men's clothes at the cliff's edge. Immediately, Superintendent Michael Curley of Salthill Garda Station launched an emergency land, sea and air search, including a search by the subaqua team. But despite an intensive search that lasted many hours, no body was ever recovered. In the days and weeks that followed, no one was reported missing and the abandoned clothes were never claimed.

It seemed as though the main suspect in Emer's murder had committed suicide and so the investigation into her death hit a major stumbling block. However, local officers soon revised their opinion and came to believe that the man had staged his suicide in a bid to divert the attention of the gardaí.

On reflection, most local gardaí felt that the man's appearance on the clifftop days earlier had been a well-staged plan, devised by the man to convince others that he was intent on taking his own life. In abandoning his clothes on the cliff and apparently vanishing from the face of the earth, the killer thought he would dupe the police and escape conviction. No doubt, he believed the investigation would hit a blockade and that gardaí would pull back on the resources being used to look into Emer's case. What this man didn't bargain for was that not everyone believed the scene he left behind.

The modus operandi of the main suspect in Emer's murder eerily mirrored the story of wife killer Colin Whelan, which was being covered heavily in news reports at the time as he was on trial. After murdering his wife in 2001, Whelan had faked his own suicide when he was on bail, by parking his car near the sea in Dublin. He had then cashed in his wife's life insurance policy before absconding to Spain where he had lived under an assumed identity until a tourist spotted him one day working in a pub and contacted the Irish police.

Some gardaí feel that Whelan's story may have been the source of inspiration behind the stunt on Dún Aengus. To date, the suspect, who hails from a small village on the coast of Connemara has not been seen. Already known to gardaí, he had a series of convictions for violent assault and was a long-term drug addict.

The fact that he could be alive and well and walking around in the belief that he has 'got away' with Emer's murder causes heartache to the her family. Emer's brother, Raymond, who still lives in Ennistymon where Emer grew up, prays every day that gardaí will knock on his door to say that they have their man. 'She was a friend more than a sister,' he says. 'You could say anything to her and she'd take it with a pinch of salt. Whether I was slagging her off or being serious with her, she'd still laugh it off. Nothing bothered her. Over the years, we fought like hell but five minutes later, we were back to normal. She was a very loving person, always smiling, and a very hard worker. Her college life meant everything to her. She had just been accepted into the National College of Art and Design in Dublin and she was really looking forward to going up to Dublin in September. She was so happy. And at the time of her murder she had so much to look forward to.'

Raymond says Emer was a very natural person. He thinks some people may have thought that she was a bit false because she was always smiling, but says she wasn't, she just genuinely saw the good in everything and everyone. She had loved art from a very young age and was always drawing. Her bedroom was always full of her pictures, many of which were self-portraits. He remembers how Emer could use her art to reflect her mood—if she was having a bad day, it was apparent in her drawings, in the darker shades she used. This was the only way her family knew that she wasn't her usual happy self. 'She was always drawing or bending and twisting pieces of paper trying to make something,' Raymond says. 'We might look at paper twisted up and thrown on the street and think of it as litter whereas Emer would stare at it and somehow see it as an arty form, an unusual design. It's only since she died that I am beginning to understand how she thought—I am only starting to get into her head. Now when I look at her paintings, even the really unusual ones, I can see what she was thinking. I couldn't see it back then, I used to just slag her over them. But I have a different attitude now. I suppose I just took her for granted when she was here and now everything she did, all her paintings, mean so much more to me. They're part of her and they're all we have left of her.'

Raymond regrets not spending more time with his little sister before her death but his memories of her will always remain with him. He remembers the last time he saw her well. 'It was about a month before she was killed. She was on work experience and she used to call in to see myself and the lads. I have three kids but only two of them were old enough to know her. She'd call in and Marie, my wife, would make a cup of tea and Emer would sit down for a chat. She was always in a rush, always someone to see or somewhere to go. She loved my kids and she'd take them out to the back garden and draw pictures for them and just mess about with them. Two of the children remember her but my youngest little girl was too small to remember her auntie, though she does recognise her in photos.

'The kids are at the age now where they keep asking questions about what happened to Emer. They'll ask about where she is now and why she doesn't come to visit any more. My little girl has been asking lately how her auntie Emer died, and I can't answer her. It's too hard to tell her how and why she will never see her again. So I just say to her that I'll tell her when she's a bit older. Our older boy says to me, "But I'm seven now, will you tell me when I'm eight?" I know in time I will have to tell them, and I know it will probably be hard for them, but, at the moment, it's just too hard for me to tell them the truth. I think it's time enough when they're in their teens. Hopefully, they'll understand a bit more then, even though it's hard enough for me to understand, because there is so much we don't know. So much the gardaí haven't told us. And that's hard. I know they have to keep certain stuff to themselves, in case they catch the person who did this, but it's hard not really knowing.'

Raymond remembers vividly the day he answered his phone and heard that his sister was missing. He says that, even then, he never for one moment thought that she could be dead.

'My father rang me to tell me that Emer was missing and I said, "What do you mean by missing?" He said, "She's missing from up where she lives and the caravan, the mobile home that was beside hers was on fire this morning and they think she was in it but they're not sure." I couldn't believe it. I told him I would head back home. My father was there when I arrived and, by then, he had heard that there was a body found in the caravan and they thought it was Emer, but they weren't sure. I had never been to the field where she lived before but we got into the car and headed off. I knew the road it was on and we got there at about 11 p.m.'

When they arrived, the scene had been sealed off but they could still walk around the side to where Emer had lived. Raymond went to see Shane, who explained that he had been at work all day and that he didn't know where Emer was. Raymond walked around the area and he saw his sister's car and her dogs. It was then that he knew it was Emer's body that was in the caravan. 'I knew that if she had gone off walking, she would have taken the dogs with her,' he says, 'and there was no way she wouldn't have come back home by 11 p.m. or wouldn't have rung someone to say where she was. I knew by looking at the dogs that they were uneasy. The dog that she always had with her was just lying there, though he was the type of dog that would normally be jumping up at you, he was a friendly thing, but that night he had his head down, tail down and he was just moping around the place.'

Raymond remembers having a gut feeling when he arrived at the site that his sister was dead. But despite his fear, he still expected her to walk through the gate at any time. He waited on the site until the early hours of the morning in the hope that something would turn up and lead them to believe that she was still alive and well. 'At 5 a.m., I left because I just couldn't stick it anymore. I just had to get out of there. I phoned the house and I asked Marie's mother, Trisha, to come down and get me. My brother drove me to Corofin and she met me there. I knew that I should have stayed on, but I just couldn't be there. I had an awful feeling about me when I was up at the site. It was as if there was something pushing me out of the place, but yet at the same time when I was leaving, something was telling me to stay. When I got home I had a cup of tea and slept for about ten minutes. I got up again and I just knew that I had to go back. Fair play to Trisha, she drove me back up again. And herself, Marie and myself just waited.

'I had a feeling that Emer was around me saying, "I'm here, but I'm not here." It sounds mad but I am convinced she was with me in the field that night. I never believed in spirits or anything like that until this happened, but I genuinely felt that she was around me. I couldn't explain it at the time and I still can't explain it now. I often wondered if she was warning me that there was something wrong. That she didn't just die in a fire, that she had been killed before. When we heard that it was Emer's remains they had found, it was like a knife had been stuck into me. We all felt it was Emer from that night ourselves, but when they tell you for definite, you just feel sick. All we wanted was to know how, why, who did it. We just couldn't understand how anyone could kill such a lovely innocent person. Why they would have wanted to kill her because she was such a nice young woman.'

In spite of his grief for his sister, Raymond is thankful to Emer for one thing—since her death, he has become very close to their older sister, Pam, who lives in the UK. Their bond, he believes, has been strengthened by the desire to get justice for Emer and to see the person responsible for her death eventually brought to court.

'None of us were close as kids, but Emer's death has changed everything. Since it happened, myself and Pam have talked for hours on the phone and Pam has come over more than ever. I have never been to visit her in England, but she visits us here all the time now. My kids love her and I know that Emer is up there pushing us together so we can get to the bottom of all this.

'When Pam came home on the day after it happened and she came over and hugged me, I knew there and then that Emer was with us and that she wanted us to become close and help her get her message across, help her get justice. It's a sad state of affairs that it took our sister's murder to bring us together, but it did. Our parents separated years ago and we all just went our separate ways but this has brought us back together again. When Pam and I talk now we keep going over the same things in our heads, asking the same questions. I believe that Emer has brought us together so that we can push and push until we find the person who did this to her. It's up to us to get justice for our sister now. We don't want her file to be just thrown in a box in a garda station gathering dust. If we don't fight for her, who will?'

Pam put together a piece that is now on YouTube with photos of Emer as a young child, growing up through her teens and into adulthood. The site has generated a lot of interest and the family hope that it will encourage someone who knows more than they pretend, to come forward and report what they know to the gardaí.

'We need the gardaí to start actively searching for this guy. We don't want to hear that he's walking around as if nothing has happened. If he has killed once, he could kill again. The problem we have is that there are new gardaí coming to our station in Ennistymon all the time and they don't know the background of Emer's case. So, when you go up there to see if anything has happened, they don't know what you're talking about and they have to read up on the case. That's very hard for us as a family. In reality, Emer's is just another statistic to the gardaí. Just another murder. But she's our sister, our flesh and blood, and we won't stop until they find who did this to her, who took her life and left her to burn in that caravan. There are people out there who know where this fella is and if they have any conscience at all, they should come forward and tell the guards what they know. Our sister won't rest in peace until he is captured and behind bars.

'The way it is now, he could be standing beside you or me on the street and no one would know who he was or what he had done. We don't want to see it happening to somebody else, and we don't want people to forget about our sister either. What we're trying to do is give her the respect that she deserves and get this file closed. Her soul will never rest and I know it won't, until he's caught and put to jail. I want him named and shamed and put in jail and if he is dead, and I know a few people believe he did take his life that day on the cliff, I want the gardaí to name him. I don't see why they can't do that if they know he did it and he's dead. It seems very unfair. In my heart, I know he's out there. I know he is alive and I want to make sure that he's found. I know once they do that Emer will be happy and she will let me know that in some way. I firmly believe that.'

―――

Pam was at her home in the UK when news came through that her little sister was missing presumed dead. It was something that she never expected to hear. However, to this day, she hasn't been able to shed a tear for the sister who idolised her as a role model.

'I haven't been able to cry since it happened,' she says. 'I just can't show any form of emotion and I really don't know why. Initially, when I was told what had happened, it was a huge shock and I think I roared, but that was the last emotional feeling I had about the whole thing. Even at the graveside, watching her coffin go into the ground, I was numb. I knew what had happened, I understood what had happened, I wasn't blanking it out but I just couldn't feel anything.'

Three years on, Pam still hasn't cried. She is able to talk about Emer's murder openly, without emotion and without any sort of reaction. To her, it feels strange, as if something is stopping her from grieving properly. She doesn't think she will grieve until her sister's killer is caught, maybe then all the emotion will come out.

Pam has previously worked as a nurse and has seen many people grieve—but there is a difference between the grief she has witnessed in her job and the grief she feels for her sister. 'The people I have dealt with through work have grieved because they had been through an illness with their loved ones, whereas Emer's death was out of the blue, totally unexpected. If it had been a car accident or something like that, at least there'd be a reason for her dying, but I think that because there's no reason, there's no grief yet.'

'You hear stories like this on the news and read them in the papers, but you never think it will happen to you. And at the time you ask yourself how these people cope, but you just have to. You don't accept it, but you have to try and get on with your life. When something like this happens to a family, it can tear you apart. Everyone reacts in a different way to try and cope with the grief. I try to keep myself busy, but I will never accept what happened until the day that man is caught, arrested and behind bars. But, even then, I'll still be asking why. Why Emer of all people? You try to go over the day in your head to get a picture of what may have happened but it's hard to understand it.

If the pope had not died when he did, Emer would have been in college and still alive today. For some reason, the power supply to their mobile home was gone, and they had a cable running from their mobile home up to the caravan where she was found. Whether she went there to investigate why the power was off, whether she went up to ask to use the electricity supply for some reason or whether she was dragged up there, no one knows—except the person who murdered her.

It's a mystery and it may be something we'll never find out. At the time that I was notified, she hadn't even been formally identified. My brother, John, came to England to tell me what had happened and all he could basically say was, "Emer is missing, there's been a fire and they found a body." That was how I came back to Ireland—knowing just those facts. It was roughly two or three weeks before we had a formal identification, and she was only identified by her bones and the jewellery she had on her that day. They took blood samples from my mother and brother, Raymond, to check. But we might never know what actually happened on that day. I think it would help a huge amount if we did. I think it would settle our minds, because we imagine what might have happened and yet it may not be half as bad as what we are thinking in our heads. So it's all a mystery, we won't know anything until the person who did it comes forward and tells us what happened and why.'

A few weeks after her death, when all the tests had confirmed that it was Emer who had died, the O'Loughlin family went to Galway to collect her body. Pam remembers a horrible feeling that came over her when the staff wheeled out an open coffin with Emer's body inside. However, the family did not see Emer, just a bag, a very small bag. 'There was no Emer to see or to grieve over,' says Pam, 'just a small bag with what was left of her remains inside. I think this was hard for us all—that we couldn't look at our sister and my father couldn't see his daughter. The person who killed Emer took that away from us. We were allowed to put things into the coffin so we put some notes from her friends and some flowers. It was the most beautiful wicker woven coffin I have ever seen, absolutely beautiful. She would have loved it! As silly as that sounds, she would have thought it was fantastic. It was a traditional woven coffin and just this tiny, tiny little body in this box. It's difficult to come to terms with the fact that she is dead because we never got the chance to see her, there was nothing to even identify her, so we had to rely on DNA. And we just have to accept that it is our sister and try and come to terms with that.'

The family brought Emer back to her parent's home to wake her. They had a police escort all the way and the tiny town where Emer had grown up gathered to say their last goodbyes. Pam slept on the floor that night, near her little sister and says she had the most relaxing few hours sleep, knowing that Emer was at rest beside her. 'I went out like a light. It was very strange. But I just felt at ease knowing that she was home with us.'

The next day was a dreadful one for the family because they had to take Emer's body to the church, though Pam didn't want to leave her sister there. Pam had started to question her faith and

Anthony Campbell's pals surround his coffin to say a last goodbye. (© *Irish Times*)

Friends and neighbours of Anthony Campbell sign a book of condolences at Greek Street Flats, Dublin. (© *Collins Photo Agency*)

Donna Cleary and her baby, Clayton.

Young Donna on her first day in school.

Donna enjoying a drink on a night out with her doting dad, Peter.

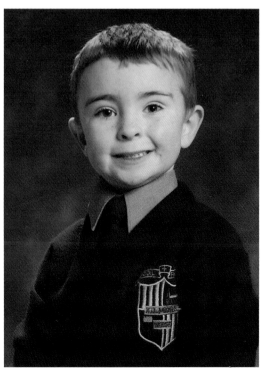

Donna's son, Clayton, aged 5.

Jeffrey Hannan's family said he always had a smile on his face.

Jeffrey with his older sister, Emily, and younger brother, Alan.

Jeffrey and Emily with their grandparents.

Jeffrey with his little girl, Nikita. He never got to see his unborn daughter, Tianna.

Patrick, Edward and Adrian Ward as little boys.

Jodie and Edward on their wedding day.

Edward had a love for horses
from the time he was a child.

Edward Ward and his first daughter, Jessica.

Sheola Keaney was always known as the life and soul of the party and people said her smile would light up a room. (© *Provision*)

Sheola's boyfriend, Thomas Kennedy, outside the Central Criminal Court in Dublin after being formally charged with her murder. (© *Press Association Images*)

The coffins of Ciara Dunne and her two little girls, Lean and Shania, being carried to their final resting place. (© *Irish Times*)

Adrian and Ciara Dunne and their children in happier times. No one could have imagined
what fate awaited them. (© *Press Association Images*)

Emer O'Loughlin was a budding artist who loved being close to nature.

Even as a young girl, Emer had a love of animals and nature.

The handmade coffin specially designed by Emer's friends and covered in rose petals.

Despite his stressful job, Brian always put the safety of his wife and children first.

Brian Stack was proud to be a senior prison officer.

As soon as he came home from work, Brian would get into his shorts
and take his sons out into the garden to play hurling.

Brian and Sheila loved to get away from it all with regular trips to the seaside with the children.

was having difficulty accepting her sister's death as God's will. 'I hated leaving her in that cold horrible place overnight. At that stage, I was finding it hard to believe that there was a God. I felt that if there was one, He wouldn't have let this happen. In my mind, there'd be loads of other ways to take her, but not this way, not being killed and burned. The only thing we can hope is that she was dead when the fire was lit. It goes through your head all the time. You keep wondering how it happened, how she managed to end up where she did and when she actually died. You just hope that she was dead before he did anything to her because the thoughts of her suffering is a nightmare. She was so fragile.'

Just like Raymond, Pam hadn't been very close to her sister. Their lives were quite disparate and as Pam was living in the UK, they didn't have the opportunity to sit down and talk like most siblings.

'I left my home in Clare when I was very young,' says Pam, 'and I hadn't seen Emer for a while. We met again at a family wedding a few years ago and I couldn't believe how grown up she had become. It was the first time, we'd spoken to each other as adults. She looked great. She was dancing with this big smile on her face. It was so different seeing her as an adult because all of my memories of her were as a child. She had come over to visit me when she was about ten and we had a great week. I brought her around the city to show her all of the sights and she loved it. She looked up to me as her big sis and thought I was great because I had a motorbike. She told everyone at home about the holiday. I just wished that there had been more times like that.'

Even though they didn't speak often, Pam was aware of what Emer was doing in her life and was very proud of the woman she had become. She remembers what a gentle, beautiful person Emer was and how much she enjoyed her art. 'She was like me in many ways, unconventional, but the difference between us was that she actually followed her dreams, she lived the artistic way out in the open, drawing all the time and she loved nature. Whereas that's something I never did and now, looking back, I regret not following my dreams.'

Pam's artistic streak was more musical, whereas her brothers enjoyed the outdoors more—but they all knew how much Emer loved art, and how she never gave up on her dream. Part of the family's sadness is that Emer's life was going really well when she was killed. She was looking forward to going to college in Dublin and building a house with her boyfriend. She had a lot to look forward to and many plans and dreams.

———

What is known of Emer's last day is that she would not have gone to the caravan in which she died of her own accord. According to people the family has spoken to, Emer was quite wary of the person who lived there. Pam doesn't think she would have gone there willingly, especially by herself as she doesn't think Emer liked the man who lived in the caravan as he had a reputation.

Emer's family worry about her last moments and wonder if she suffered before she died. Their hope is that she died quickly and without pain but they may never know for certain, if the murderer is never found. At the time of Emer's murder, some local people blamed her lifestyle for her death, something that irritates Pam.

'Living where she did, in a mobile home in a field, she was isolated. Nobody would have heard her cry, nobody would have heard her scream and nobody would have seen what happened. At the time, we heard through small-town gossip that people were blaming Emer's death on her lifestyle, but it didn't matter what her lifestyle was, she didn't deserve the death she got. And our family didn't deserve what happened to her either. If she'd had lived in a town, in a flat maybe, it wouldn't have happened but then people are murdered in towns and cities all the time. It really annoys and hurts me when I hear that some people half-blame Emer herself for living the artistic lifestyle she did in a mobile home, hoping to build a house on that site, it's very unfair. Shane and Emer actually had the foundation timbers already bought for the house and they were looking forward to getting started on their new home. There's a cross on the site now, built with that very wood, which marks the spot where she was killed. That's very hard to take. She died at the hands of someone who must have had something seriously wrong with him. He left her in such a horrible way and it's that person who people should be talking about, not analysing how my sister lived. It's very hurtful for us all.'

The family's hopes are pinned on the gardaí keeping their investigation open to find Emer's killer. As far as the guards are concerned, hers is an open, unsolved murder case that's still being actively investigated. Interpol are involved, as are the British police force. The gardaí are trying to involve as many police forces and agencies as they possibly can in their efforts to catch the person who killed this fun-loving young woman. The family have had assurances from the guards that they're not going to go away, they're not going to forget about this. 'That was my one fear,' says Pam, 'more than anything else. That it would be forgotten about, that it would just drift into the background and Emer would just be consigned to a filing cabinet somewhere as a 'cold case' but we've been assured that that's most certainly not the case.'

Gardaí have confirmed that they believe the chief suspect in Emer's murder is still alive and that the clothes left on the side of the cliff on Inis Mór were part of a staged suicide. The gardaí are following several leads—although the family is not given many details—and are very much still looking for Emer's killer, who doesn't seem to have persuaded many people that he is dead. The family's hope now is that someone who knows this man, knows what he did and knows where he is now, will come forward and tell the gardaí what they know in confidence. It is the only way the family think they will get some justice for Emer.

Emer's mother, Josephine, was too ill to go to Galway for the release of her daughter's body. Her family thought it better for her to stay in her flat in Dublin until they had Emer home with them. But it hurts Josephine to know that she wasn't there for her daughter's final journey home.

'I still can't accept what happened to her,' says Josephine, 'but it would have been easier, I think, if we'd had a body to bury. How can any of us know what was in that coffin, what was buried. It could have been stones or sand for all we know. In my heart, I don't feel she got a proper burial because of how she was found. There are days when I am very angry and days when I am placid, but my feelings are all over the place.'

Josephine says she can be in her flat for days on end because she doesn't feel she has a right to be here on earth, walking around, when her daughter is gone. And yet she has to deal with the fact that the man who killed her daughter is also walking around freely. She finds it hard.

Emer is in Josephine's thoughts every day. The day she heard her daughter had been killed was the worst of her life and she will never forget it. 'I was sitting in my flat and young John, my son, kept ringing and ringing and he kept saying that he was coming up to Dublin to tell me something. He asked me if there was anyone there with me because he didn't want to tell me what he had to tell me on my own. So I said I would get one of my friends over. I couldn't understand what could have been so bad that he needed to come up to Dublin, all the way from Clare, to tell me face to face.

'I remember I was sitting on the side of the bed and he knelt down in front of me. I was just glued to the bed and he just told me straight out that Emer was missing and they were sure that she had burned in this fire. I was just numb. I kept asking him how it happened, why it happened. Of course he wasn't able to tell me anything, because he didn't even know himself. He said he had to come up to Dublin because he didn't want to tell me over the phone, he didn't want the police coming to my door and he was hoping to get to me before I heard something on the news.'

John stayed with his mother for about an hour, before he caught a flight to England to tell his sister, Pam. Josephine knows it was a very hard thing for him to have to do and she is proud of him for how he handled what was happening. Josephine says it took about three days for the news to sink in. Like everyone else, she had heard of such things on the news, when they happen to other people, but she never thought it was something that could ever happen to her, because in her mind all of her children are good people.

'Emer deserves justice,' says Josephine. 'She came into the world like a tiger and went out like a lamb. She was a little fighter. I had a very hard pregnancy on Emer but as she grew up, I was so proud of her. I always knew she would have a good life and that she would do well. When you give birth, you never know how your children will turn out, but I knew from a young age that she was a fighter and she'd get what she wanted from life.'

Like every mother and daughter, Emer and Josephine had their disagreements at times, but Emer never held a grudge. She did well in school and always had lots of friends. Her mother knows that Emer would have done well after college if she had not been killed.'

Now all Josephine has left are her memories and thoughts of what her daughter went through. 'It's hard to get through a day without thinking of what happened and I've had people come up to me and say that they'd love to talk to me but they just don't know what to say. But we just have to get through this as best we can. I haven't gone to counselling to be honest because to me it would just be accepting what happened and I'm not prepared to do that. I'll never accept it until that man is caught. So I feel by going to counselling I would be only throwing in the towel and I can't do it. You just don't give up, you can't afford to.

'Her death was so vicious. It was the worst death imaginable and my family are now living a life sentence with this hanging over us. I'm not happy with the way things are going with the investigation. The police are saying, "We're trying to do this and we're doing that" but when you're sitting back and you see that there's nothing being done, it's very frustrating. It's all being said, but nothing is happening. But we just have to hang on in there and wait and see what the outcome is.'

———

For Emer's boyfriend, Shane, things are as difficult as they are for the rest of her family. He still lives in the mobile home he shared with the girl he fell in love with when he was only 17 years old. He still prays that her murderer will one day be caught and he tries to get on with his life as best he can by holding on to the many memories he has of the love of his life.

'I first met Emer when I was about 12 or 13 when I was on summer holidays in Ennistymon. I used to go down there every summer and I knew her on and off for years. When I was about 17, we became good friends and it just sort of took off from there, we didn't look back really. We just got on really well. We were best friends for years before we ever had a relationship. It just worked. I think that in the five years we were together we spent only ten or 15 days apart. We were very close.'

Shane talks of the Emer he knew as a shy person in many ways, though she was very happy. He says she loved to sit back and watch everybody else, see what they were doing and get her own view of things. They had a good life. They moved in together because Shane had to move out of the place he was living in—so they gave living together a go.

'Emer was the type of person who loved to have nice little things around her, bits of art and things. She was very artistic. And she did a lot for me. I came from Galway city and she just helped me get out of a lot of stuff myself, get my head together, stop messing about, she helped me get my life back on track really.'

The couple lived together for about six or seven months before they decided they wanted to leave County Clare for a while—so they went to Holland. They lived there for two years, working in factories, which they found tedious at times, but a good experience as well. They were able to save money more easily when they were there and they respected the money they had. Their accommodation was paid for and they didn't have any bills at the end of the week, so they managed to save some cash. They returned to Ireland for a while and then headed over to Thailand for three months. 'My best memories now are of the time we spent together in Thailand, it was just free time, the best holiday we ever really had, doing whatever we wanted to do and it was just a ball really.'

When the couple arrived back in County Clare after their trip to Thailand, they decided to get a mobile home and 'put their heads down' for a couple of years. Emer had got a place in college and Shane was working. Life was going well for them.

'We had plans to build a house,' says Shane, 'and things were going well. Emer was nearly finished her first year in college and I was working with a guy on the building sites at the time. But Emer's education was a priority, so if she had moved to college in Dublin, we would have figured a way around it, or maybe I would have moved to Dublin. I don't know really what would have happened, but we would have just taken it as it came.' Shane is proud of the life he and Emer built together and of the plans they had for their future. They chose to live their lives the way they wanted and were practical in planning for their future. 'We decided to live this kind of life, in a mobile home, because I had the land and rent is crazy, so we thought that if we invested in a mobile home we could live here rent free, work and save to do other things, instead of putting all our money into rent. A mortgage was the last thing we wanted, we didn't want to sign our lives away to a bank. So we kind of saw a way out of that by living on the land and we decided to give it a go and see how we got on. And it was working fine.

'She was so happy living here. She loved her dogs, she loved nature and she loved living in such a peaceful, quiet place. It was a really good time in her life. After work we'd come home, listen to music, Emer might draw and I'd probably be working with some wood or carving something and then we'd watch a movie. We had a routine, every day I'd go to Lisdoonvarna, she'd go to Galway and when we'd get home we'd cook the dinner and do our bits and pieces and then chill out. I miss all that.' On the day Emer died, Shane left their mobile home at about 9 a.m. He remembers that there was no electricity that morning and that Emer had said she would go to one of the neighbours if she needed power. Shane says she was in good form and nothing seemed out of the ordinary.

Early that afternoon, he answered a call on his mobile phone, saying that his neighbour's caravan was on fire. One of his colleagues drove him back to the site and although nothing had been mentioned about Emer, he had a feeling in his stomach that something just wasn't right.

'I had a bad feeling when I was leaving, it just didn't sound good from the phone call I got. When I got there, the dogs were running wild and Emer's car was there. The doors of our mobile and the car were open which was unusual—Emer was the kind of person who always locked her car, even outside the shop in the local town. The dogs were always taken care of as well, so it was odd to see them running about. The doors were swinging open and Emer wasn't to be seen. So we hoped that she had gone somewhere to phone about the fire or something.'

Shane and a neighbour went over to where the fire was and saw what they thought were human remains in the ashes, at first they presumed they belonged to the man who owned the caravan. By this stage, the local garda had arrived. Shane says that when Emer didn't show up after a while, everyone knew pretty quickly that the remains may have been hers. He had a gut feeling that something was wrong.

'When there was no sign of Emer coming back, I phoned her father and told him what had happened and he was down as quickly as he could,' says Shane. 'All that was left of the caravan by that stage was a burned chassis. There was nothing else left, all the aluminium was gone, it had all just melted down. There was absolutely nothing, just a black wreck. We could make out some weights and burned cutlery, but all the glass was gone. I had a sickening feeling all that day that it was Emer whose remains were in the caravan.

'When she didn't come back that evening, I knew it was her. I had hoped that she had gone off to get help but the longer she was away, the more I realised it was bad.'

No one really knows what happened that morning. It is believed that Emer left the mobile home she shared with Shane with her phone and charger in order to find somewhere to charge her phone to call Shane. But something happened when she got to her neighbour's mobile home.

Gardaí found her mobile phone in the wreckage but her charger was never found. However, it is widely believed that someone was in the caravan when Emer called because she was the type of person who liked her privacy and so she respected other people's privacy. Shane says she would never have gone into someone's home if they had not been there and if she had not been asked in.

The family were all questioned after the fire. Shane wasn't surprised to be questioned and was happy to help in any way he could. Everyone in the family helped the guards as much as they could. 'Any time they asked me in,' says Shane, 'I was there willing to help, to give whatever information about myself or anybody I knew to the guards. So they could use it or not use it, so they could eliminate whatever they had to eliminate or use whatever they could to try and patch things together. I suppose they are looking at it from a completely outsider's view, they don't know anybody so they have to get to know everyone in question.'

Everyone knows that the main suspect was Shane and Emer's next-door neighbour. Shane says the man always came across as a straight-up kind of guy, but that he never really got to know him. Shane does admit though that Emer didn't trust the man and he says it's a pity that he didn't listen to her instincts. 'I just wanted to keep it friendly between the neighbours,' he says. 'I didn't want to cause any trouble, I just wanted to be a friendly neighbour.'

Shane remembers that on the morning of the murder, he had told Emer to charge her phone at the neighbours', but that Emer didn't want to. He had told her that she'd be fine. He knows that was probably a mistake, but says that you don't think of these things before they happen. That you can't imagine something like this happening to anyone you know. He never thought anything could happen to Emer.

'I miss Emer with all my heart every day. I say hello to her every morning and I say goodnight to her every night. She's part of my life, she's what keeps me going. She's the reason I probably haven't completely cracked because I knew her so well. We'd lost a few friends together over the years and we had comforted their relatives by trying to tell them how to live the way our friends, who had lost their lives, would have wanted them to live. I knew Emer so well and I know she wouldn't want me to waste my life after her life was already wasted. So I've tried to live my life since as best I can and remember her as well as I can and just try and take some good out of what's happened.'

Shane and a friend erected a cross in Emer's memory at the site where she died. It was made from an oak sleeper that the couple had planned to use in the frame of their new home. Shane worked hard to clean up the area where the fire took hold and he has managed to restore the site.

'I've stayed on here in the mobile home because it was our home and I don't believe in running from anything. I feel like I had to stay here and try and carry on with the life that we had. I stayed because I like it here and I know that Emer is here, her spirit is here all around me and I'll probably always stay here. But every day is difficult.

'I do believe that the chief suspect in this case is still alive. His body has never been found. His clothes were found folded neatly on top of Dún Aengus. I don't think we have any proof that he's still alive, but I still believe firmly that he is. I'm very angry at times; angry that Emer's life has been wasted for no reason whatsoever and just as she had started to blossom in her schoolwork and started to do what she wanted to do. She was really making something of herself and her life was robbed. It's like an open book. We're still sitting here wondering what's going to happen or what will be done. Will we ever find out what happened? It would be nice to close the case, at least we could know that everything was done and know that Emer's killer has been caught. Maybe then we could have peace of mind.'

Retired Detective Inspector Brian Sherry believes that there are evil people in our society who have no remorse for their crimes. These are people who can murder someone and never have a moment of guilt. Throughout his career, he has been face to face with people who have savagely attacked and killed innocent victims and who know the law better than some lawyers. But he also knows that there are some killers who try to copy murders they have seen on television, believing that they won't get caught. But, inevitably, they make some mistake so that they can be prosecuted and be put behind bars.

'I have been asked many times if people who commit murder are smarter than the average criminal,' he says, 'but I honestly don't believe they are. I've met people who think they've committed the perfect crime and yet when you go and start investigating it, you'll find that they've made a mistake somewhere along the line; that they haven't covered all the angles. A lot of the people who are committing crimes nowadays are looking at the *csi* (*Crime Scene Investigation*) programmes dealing with forensic investigations and they are very forensic conscious. For example, they go out and they buy rubber gloves and rubber suits and everything else that they see murderers wear on television to commit crime and then they make the most basic of mistakes and they leave themselves wide open.

Programmes like *csi* are definitely educating the criminal but, there again, every time you serve a Book of Evidence on a criminal here in Dublin, you're educating them. Books of Evidence which contain all the evidence that the state is going to produce in the course of a criminal trial against a suspect are passed around certain pubs in certain parts of the city every Saturday and every Sunday and you have 'the barstool barristers' talking about the best way they can defend themselves, get themselves out of their situations. That said, investigating officers will do everything they can to convict someone whom they know for definite carried out a murder. They will leave no stone unturned in an effort to get a conviction. And whilst it can be very hard for families not to know everything about their son's or daughter's murder, it is crucial that any incriminating evidence is kept firmly under wraps until such time as it comes to court. But it's very hard for the families who have been waiting for years for answers.'

The formation of the Cold Case Unit means that there are ways and means to look at a case, even years after it has happened. The guards in this unit will come to a case with a completely fresh and totally different view. But the actions of the gardaí are not always quick enough for the family of the murdered person.

'Closure is very important for the family of a murdered person. It doesn't take away from the pain and the suffering they feel, but it does help. It's very important for them to see someone brought to justice. More than anything they want to know that their loved one's life hasn't been taken in vain,' says Brian Sherry. 'It is, therefore, hard for families who have never seen anyone brought to court and charged—and sentenced—for taking the life of a loved one. In some cases, the relatives of the victim know the person who is responsible for the murder, they also know that the gardaí know who's responsible for the murder themselves and yet they can't have any closure because they haven't got that one vital piece of information and evidence.'

Generally, the guards liaise with victims' families during the course of the investigation, keeping them as much appraised of events as they possibly can. But, obviously, when every avenue is exhausted and there are new murders taking place and various serious crimes happening, you can't devote all of your time to the one investigation.

'It's something that is hard for families to understand at times, and that's only natural. But what families have to know is that the file is never closed, it's still there, always there. Unfortunately, the problem is that it's not always humanly possible to crack a case.

'You try and convince the families that you're doing your best but, sometimes, it takes longer than you think. In cases where the investigation leads you overseas, it can be very difficult to get through myriads of red tape. This happens a lot when you are dealing with other police forces and governments. But when a case is open, it can change any day. Today, there may be nothing to act on, but tomorrow someone could come forward or you could receive a phone call out of the blue and everything changes. And that is the hope that every family has to try to hold on to. That one day something small may happen that will change the whole course of the investigation and lead to an arrest and, eventually, a conviction.

'As a detective, there is nothing you want more than to be able to knock on the door and tell a family that you have finally got the break you needed in the case to make an arrest. It is the best feeling you can have—to see the relief on their faces. No matter how complicated the case may seem, no matter how little evidence there may be, there is always the chance of a breakthrough and although it may be very hard at times, families must always hold on to that hope.'

06 | KILLED BY JEALOUSY
SHEOLA KEANEY

On the evening of Sunday, 16 July 2006, gardaí found the body of 19-year-old Sheola Keaney wrapped in black and green plastic bin bags, hidden underneath a pile of metal bars and hedge-clippings, down a laneway at a place called Newtown in Cobh, County Cork.

Dressed in only her panties and a bra, Sheola was found to have traces of semen on her underwear and on her genitalia. It was obvious that whoever had killed her so brutally had also had sexual intercourse with her before abandoning her bruised and bloodied body in the dense undergrowth.

A post-mortem examination later revealed that the stunning six foot blonde waitress, who had been missing for three days, had died from asphyxia brought about by manual strangulation.

Sheola had disappeared from a barbecue in the early hours of Saturday, 14 July. She had been at the party with her pals and throughout the night, she had received a number of text messages from her ex-boyfriend, 21-year-old Thomas Kennedy from Russell Heights in Cobh. At around 3.30 a.m., she left the barbecue and headed off to meet Kennedy. She told friends that he was a bit worried about something and he wanted to talk.

Kennedy and Sheola had been in a turbulent relationship for

about 18 months and her father, Peter, had warned her on several occasions to distance herself from her over-jealous boyfriend before things got completely out of hand.

In the months and weeks before her death, she had made numerous phone calls and sent dozens of text messages to her dad, asking him to tell Kennedy to leave her alone. According to Peter, Kennedy's behaviour was becoming more and more intolerant. He would regularly lose his temper, even in front of their friends, and would threaten Sheola, or degrade her by telling her that she was fat and ugly.

Peter believed that Kennedy was making his daughter's life hell and he knew that, even though they had split up, Kennedy was still hanging around. Peter feared that if Sheola continued to meet up with him, as had been happening, things could turn very sour. Though he never for one minute thought it would end in her murder.

———

When Sheola Keaney came into the world on 22 January 1987, her parents Carol and Peter were overjoyed. She was the first—and only—child born to the young couple who were only starting out on their life's journey together.

Sheola's arrival on a cold winter's day at Erinvile Hospital turned their lives around and just seven months later, Peter and Carol married in Cobh surrounded by family, friends and their baby daughter.

The family soon moved back to Clonmel, where Peter was working, and lived there for nearly 11 years. Unfortunately, things didn't work out between Carol and Peter and the couple eventually separated. Peter continued living in their three-bedroom home and Carol moved back to the picturesque village of Cobh, 110 kilometres away.

Both Carol and Peter had grown up in the beautiful Cork village and both still had family in the area. Sheola, who was in sixth class in the Sisters of Charity primary school in Clonmel at the time, initially went with her mother to live in Glenenaar in Cork and attended St Mary's National School in Cobh. However, Peter went to court seeking joint custody and, months later, Sheola returned to Tipperary where she started school in Rockwell College in Cashel, one of the most prestigious private colleges in Ireland.

Peter recalls how his little girl with her unusual blue-green eyes turned his life around and left a lasting impression with everyone who came into contact with her.

'She was the best gift that I ever got,' he says. 'I can't even describe in words the feeling when someone hands you a bundle of joy. The day she came into the world was definitely one of the happiest of my life. We hadn't asked the doctors whether Carol was having a boy or a girl and we were delighted when Sheola arrived, especially me, as I only had one sister growing up and I was delighted with a girl. I always thought that girls were easier to handle than boys.

'We decided to name her Sheola, an African name spelled slightly differently but which meant Mary or Marie—my mother's name was Mary and Carol's mother was Marie, so it worked out well for both sides. As a little girl, Sheola was a joy, always in good humour, she never had problems with sleeping or eating, a dream child. She was basically just a happy little kid, full of life and always on the go. Carol and myself idolised her. When I look back on pictures of her as a baby, smiling, I just can't believe that it has all happened. That she is gone from me forever.

'She was a little beauty in her First Holy Communion dress and I remember clearly on the day looking at her standing there in this lovely plain white dress and thinking how proud I was going to be when I eventually walked her down the aisle to get married. She was so special to me. When she went to Cobh for that short time with her mother, I was devastated and I thought I'd never get her back. It was a nightmare. But thank God it all worked out well and I got to spend some time with her before she was taken from me for good.

'I think the best thing I ever did was to send her to Rockwell. It made such a difference to her. I think she felt as if she had another family out there. It was a mixed school and she met people from all over the world, and all over Ireland, and the friends she made turned out to be friends for life.'

Peter says that Sheola was a very good student, her favourite subjects were English and history. Her love of sport and music came to the fore at Rockwell and she was involved in the school hockey team and the school choir. When she was at home, the house would come to life to the sound of Shakira and Eminem. And her presence was always felt around their home.

Sheola was a day border in Rockwell, she left the house at 8 a.m. and got back at about 9 p.m. By the time she got home, she would have finished all her studies and would have had something to eat so she was able to sit down with her father for a chat as he would have got home from work.

Peter remembers the great plans Sheola had for her life. Her main dream was to make some money and travel the world. He remembers how she loved packing her suitcase to head off somewhere. 'She'd been to France, Germany, Tunisia, England and all over Ireland—and she was only 19 when she died, so she was really getting about. She was a very intelligent girl, she knew what she was about and she was hilarious.'

He talks of his daughter's natural instinct to walk into a room and 'eat the room up'. By which he meant that by the time she was ready to leave, everyone would know her and she'd know everybody there. 'She had a fantastic way with people, both young and old. I always admired that about her. She was the one you could turn to if you were feeling down or lonely, because she was a great listener.'

Despite the many options Sheola had after she left school, she decided to go to college and take up business studies—she was due to start her course in the September after her death. Most of her friends had gone straight to college after the Leaving Certificate but, after talking it through with her dad, Sheola made the decision to take a gap year and get a job to help her save some money which would help her through her time at college.

Her first job was at Fota Island Golf Club and then she went on to take up a position in Rushbrooke Hotel. But she spent all of her free time with her pals, partying and enjoying life to the full.

At weekends, the Keaney house would be hectic—especially on Saturday nights, when all of Sheola's friends would come over and get ready in her room to go out. The music blared and everyone would be laughing and joking. Every weekend, the house would be turned upside down. 'I loved those times,' says Peter. 'Hearing them all in good form and having a laugh and a joke. That's how it's so hard to cope nowadays; the silence in the house eats me up. And it makes you realise that there really is no going back. That she is really gone for good. That breaks my heart. Looking back through old photos of Sheola from her early teens, it's very hard to find one of her on her own. She was always surrounded by people. She had a zest for life and she enjoyed every moment of it.' Peter thinks it might be easier to cope if Sheola had been a quieter shy girl with fewer friends.

He remembers well the last time that he saw his daughter. They spoke to each other often over the phone—even on the night she died—but the last time he had seen her was in May 2006, two months before she was so callously murdered. 'She was moving from one job to another and she had got a pay rise, she was in great form. I sat in the bar of the hotel having a pint whilst she went in for her interview and because the man interviewed her in the bar itself, I could hear everything, and I sat there laughing to myself at how she conducted the whole interview. She basically told them what she wanted and she got it. I was so proud of her that day.'

The following morning, Peter collected Sheola and took her to Fota Park so she could tell them that she was leaving. However, her employers said that they would be stuck because there was a golf classic coming up, so she agreed to work in Rushbrooke during the day and at Fota at night—that way neither of them would be stuck. She didn't want to leave anyone in the lurch.

Peter remembers his daughter as a feisty girl with a big heart, who always stuck by the rules. 'If she went out, she knew that she had to be back by a certain time,' says Peter, 'and if she was delayed, she would ring me and let me know what was happening. There was always a few of them out together, so I knew that they'd stick together and get a taxi home, so although as a parent you worry anyway, I never really had any need to worry with Sheola. She was a good girl. That's why I knew something was wrong on the day I got a call to say she hadn't turned up for work in Cork.'

It was Peter's niece who made the call in the early hours of Saturday, 14 July. She asked Peter if Sheola had decided to go back to Tipperary during the night after the party. Peter thought it strange that no one knew where she was, but he tried to rationalise things by telling himself that she might have just stayed with a friend and they hadn't contacted anyone yet. He went to work that morning with a nagging doubt in the back of his mind, whilst still hoping for the best.

'During that afternoon I got a phone call to say that things weren't looking good,' he says. 'No one could find her. So then I got really worried and I got straight into the car and started to drive to Cobh. On the way, I got a call from Tom Kennedy, Sheola's ex-boyfriend, and he asked me if I was coming down to Cobh. I told him that I wasn't, that I was in Tipperary—even though, by that stage, I was at Fota Island, just a few miles away—but I thought something was up and I didn't trust him. I asked him where he was and he said he was in the garda barracks. When I asked him why he was there, he said he was the last person to see Sheola and they were asking him questions. He said that when he was finished with the guards, he was going up to his brother's house to make up flyers to give out around the town.'

Peter then told Tom Kennedy that he would be with him in five minutes—and Kennedy's voice changed immediately. 'I could tell he was nervous and that he knew something about Sheola's disappearance. When I walked into the house, his face went white and I knew instinctively that he was the guy responsible. I knew that he'd done something to Sheola. He couldn't look at me and kept turning away while I was asking him questions. If I walked into one room, he'd walk out of it. He had guilt written all over his face. At one stage, I went out and I said to the garda sergeant,

"Look, he's the guy who done it." The guard said to me, "Look for the next few days, you'll have to keep him as close to you as possible, because if he commits suicide we'll never find her." But they did warn me that I couldn't make those sort of allegations to people, until it could be proved. I knew I had to keep my feelings to myself, but I also knew there and then that the guards were suspicious of him and that he had done it. And I knew that he had changed his story a few times, so they were watching him.'

On Saturday, 15 July, the gardaí had got in contact with the Minister for Justice at the time, Michael McDowell, to seek permission to get her mobile phone records. Tom kept asking Peter what was happening about her phone and Peter told him that even if her phone was off, they could get a signal so that they could find it. Peter could see that Kennedy was getting nervous. Although he knew that Kennedy had done something to Sheola, he found it very hard to accept. Peter knew that if he did accept it, then he was admitting to himself that his daughter was dead. That was something he couldn't do.

'I could never have imagined that Tom Kennedy would kill my daughter when I first met him. They seemed so content together at first, but, as time went on, I could see how unhappy Sheola was becoming. You would think that a lad going out with such a gorgeous girl, in every way, would be only delighted with himself. You'd think he'd want to do everything for her. But she was just too nice for him. He couldn't take it that people liked her so much. And I believe it was his jealousy that killed her in the end.'

Peter recalls how Kennedy denied knowing anything about Sheola's disappearance during his first interview with the gardaí. He told them that he had brought Sheola back to his house in the early hours of Saturday morning and that they had stayed up chatting. He stated that she had then slept in his sister's bedroom and that Sheola had left the house at around 10 a.m. and he hadn't seen her since. He spent 12 hours undergoing questioning at Cobh Garda Station. However, when he heard that DNA traces had been taken from Sheola's underwear and body for examination, he changed his story.

'He then told gardaí that Sheola and himself had sex on the morning she disappeared,' says Peter. 'Then, he claimed, that they had had some breakfast and had gone out for a walk around Newtown. As they walked along, Kennedy claimed he didn't know what came over him but he grabbed Sheola from behind, putting his left arm around her neck and tightening it with his right arm. He let go as they fell. He told gardaí that he had panicked when he realised she was dead and hid her body.'

When Kennedy was formally charged at Cobh Garda Station on the night of Friday, 21 July, his reply to Garda Sergeant Brian Goulding was, 'Plead guilty, like, I suppose.' The trial was set for December 2006 and was heard at the Central Criminal Court in Cork.

When Sheola had first started to go out with Thomas Kennedy, she was very happy. The two got on really well and he was her first long-term boyfriend, so she was excited about the relationship. They did what every young couple does and they seemed to be in love. However, as time went on, things began to change and, after a while, they were arguing all the time. Coming up to, around April and May 2006—the last few months of Sheola's life—things had become very bad between the two and Sheola wasn't happy.

The two were once at a birthday party in Killarney and Sheola's male friends who were there heard her screaming in one of the rooms. They kicked in the door and Sheola was lying on the bathroom floor crying and Kennedy was running around like a madman. Sheola's friends brought her into their room from where she rang her father. 'She told me she was iffy about the relationship,' says Peter. 'She didn't know what to do. She asked me why Kennedy was doing this to her. I wasn't happy at all with how things were between them and I just wanted her away from him.'

However, Peter didn't want Sheola to think he was being pushy and interfering, so he tried to forget about the night at the party.

Then, she rang him again. 'She rang me and said, "Look would you ring him? I was at a barbecue and he made an absolutely holy show of me." So I rang him, but he wouldn't answer his phone, so I just left a voice message telling him to ring me back. But, of course, he didn't. Then a few weeks later, they rowed again at another barbecue. He then went back to a house where Sheola was with her pals, in her mam's house, and he started screaming abuse through the door and kicking on the door. She rang me the next day and was very upset. I said, "Sheola, it's like this, you have two options. If you want to stay with this person, you stay with him, but that's what your life is going to be like. Or you can leave him for good. But you have options." And I told her that it was one thing him having no respect for her but when it came to having no respect for her mother either, then it was a different matter. He just didn't seem to care about anyone.'

Peter says Kennedy was always around and always causing trouble. Even when Sheola went out with her girl friends and he was with them, he would argue with her about men who were looking at her, calling them 'fucking gurriers'. He let her know what he would do to them for looking at her. All of this was starting to get to Sheola and she began to see that they couldn't go on anymore. 'He was starting to really get to her,' says Peter, 'and she rang me up one day and she said, "You're right. I can do better for myself." I could tell that she was very hurt because she had decided to break up with him, but she knew she had no choice. She couldn't have gone on like that any longer. It was breaking her heart.'

Sheola got attention everywhere she went—she was six foot tall with long blonde hair and model looks. She also had a magnetic personality and everyone who met her said how likeable she was. For Tom Kennedy, this was a problem. 'He couldn't handle it,' says Peter. 'I'd say she did everything in her power to give him the benefit of the doubt when he was being aggressive to her, but there was only so much she could take. She was in love and she could see no wrong in him whatsoever. If anyone passed a comment about how good she looked, he would tell her she was fat and then she'd go on a diet and lose weight. He would say he didn't like the colour of her hair and she would change it. He basically tried to control her all the time. We could all see, in the months coming up to her death, that she was losing confidence in herself. Everyone could see it. But when they split up, she moved on a bit and she started seeing another guy. But she stayed friends with Kennedy because that was the type of person she was, always wanting to keep people happy. And she seemed to be very happy.

'She rang me one night and said, "Dad I'm after meeting a guy from Cobh, nothing major going on, we're only pals at the moment." I was delighted for her—I knew both his parents and the young fellow was a very nice guy. I honestly thought this was going to turn her life around, meeting someone new and moving on. I never thought she would end up murdered.'

———

Sheola was well known around Cobh and her disappearance sparked major concern and upset within the small community. Hundreds of people took to the streets in the hope that they would find her alive and well.

'To be perfectly honest, it was one of the most frightening times of my life,' says Peter. 'Just the sheer horror of seeing so many people going different directions looking for my child and every time someone pulled up a plastic bag in a field or something from a ditch, my heart would stop, thinking she was underneath it.' I was hoping against all hope that we might find her unconscious and that we'd get her to a hospital and she'd be fine.'

However, Peter knew in his heart that something was seriously wrong—and had known from the time he first got the call to say she hadn't gone to work. 'There was no way that Sheola would have gone to work with the same clothes she'd had on from the night before,' says Peter, 'and she had my niece, Rebecca's, phone, car keys and a cash card, which she knew Rebecca needed for her own work the following morning. I knew it wasn't like Sheola not to keep in contact with her pals.'

Like most young people her age, Sheola was never without her mobile phone. Peter knows that she would have phoned him to let him know if something had happened. She had phoned him about Kennedy and the problems he was causing, regularly, so he is certain that, if she could have got to a phone, she would have rung somebody. 'So when we were searching the area,' he says, 'I had a sick feeling come over me that she was dead. It just didn't make sense, any of it.'

When Peter got to the laneway where Sheola's body had been left, he noticed that the guards had sealed off the area. He went under the tape to try and see what was happening, but a guard stopped him, telling him he couldn't go any farther. Peter told the guard that Sheola was his daughter and that he could go up the laneway if he wanted. At that point the garda told him to stay back, saying, 'There was something found.'

The guard then told Peter to go back to his brother's house, and that they would call him there if they found anything that he needed to know about.

Peter headed back to his brother's home and rang Tom Kennedy to see where he was. Kennedy told Peter that he was at home with his family. Peter snapped. 'I asked him straight out, "Where is she?" He said, "What are you on about?" I said, "If you confessed to have loved her at all, you'll put Carol and me out of our misery and let us know." And he just said, "I don't know what you're on about." I then said, "I hope you rot in hell", and I put the phone down.'

A short time later, Peter got the call he had been dreading. They had found his daughter's body.

'I had heard before this that they had found her handbag and that her shoes were in it and, sure, wherever her bag was her body wasn't going to be too far away. To be honest, once I knew the handbag was there and she had no shoes on, I knew she was dead. But I had to try and stay strong and I just kept praying she was OK. But it was very hard to do that when your heart was telling you something different. I cannot describe how I felt when I heard the garda saying that they had found the body of my child. It was like my life had just flashed before me. The worst nightmare anyone could have. I went numb. It was a sickening feeling. I think looking back on it, the hardest part for me was knowing that she had lain out there for days in the blazing heat and we never found her. And then knowing that she had to stay lying there, dead, until forensics, the state pathologist and the priest had all been with her and done whatever they needed to do.

'What really got to me was that I had walked that laneway a number of times over the previous few days looking for Sheola, but I had seen nothing. There was so much undergrowth that I didn't notice a thing. There are back gardens right where she was found but I didn't even know they were there because the ground was so overgrown.

'It killed me that I couldn't go near her, go over to her and hug her and tell her that I was sorry I wasn't there to help her, to tell her that I loved her. I had to just stay away and let these professional people do what they needed to do to put the bastard who killed her away.'

As hard as it had been for Peter to come to terms with the fact that Sheola was dead, the hardest part was seeing her in the funeral parlour on the day her body was brought back to Cobh. The undertakers had no choice but to put Sheola's body in a closed coffin, because of the extent of her injuries and the deterioration of her body because of the length of time she had spent in the open air in such intense heat. Peter says this was difficult for her extended family and friends to cope with as they could not say their final farewells face to face.

'The only ones allowed to see her were Carol, myself and some very close friends and family,' he says. 'The vision of her lying there in that box will live with me forever. To see this beautiful girl that was my daughter, lying there battered and bruised with her eyes stitched closed in the coffin made me feel sick. Even then, days later, blood was still oozing out through her ears. She was unrecognisable really. Obviously we knew it was Sheola, we knew it was our child, but it didn't look like her at all. I don't know where I got the strength from that day in the funeral parlour. It was so hard to believe that another human being could have done that to someone. The only thing we can be thankful for is that she was found and we got to say goodbye to her, unlike a lot of families who lose a child.'

However, the heartache was only starting for Peter and Carol Keaney and their families. Tom Kennedy was arraigned on Tuesday, 28 November 2006 at Mallow District Court where he pleaded not guilty to murder. The trial was to take place in the Central Criminal Court in Cork and was set to last until Christmas week. There were plans put in place to hear the evidence from over 150 witnesses.

Just one week later, on Tuesday, 5 November, Kennedy changed that plea from not guilty to guilty. He offered no explanation for his change of heart. In one way, it was a godsend for the family, as they did not have to face the trauma of hearing the horrific details of how their daughter lost her life so brutally. But the plea change caused further stress and anxiety for Peter, as he had wanted to know the full facts behind the attack and did not believe that a guilty verdict would unearth the true story behind the death of his beautiful daughter.

'I knew that once he pleaded guilty, it would not be necessary for the witnesses to come forward,' says Peter. 'And then we would never know where he had sex with Sheola, what really happened that night and what everyone saw. It killed me to think that he was getting off so lightly. I knew that once he pleaded guilty all of the evidence in the original Book of Evidence would be inadmissible. As far as I'm concerned, it was the easy way out for Kennedy, and it left us with so many unanswered questions. In my heart, I believe that he planned Sheola's murder, he didn't just do it on the spur of the moment as he claimed. He did a very good job of covering her up. I was disgusted with how he even went home to get bin bags to cover her feet up. Her feet were in a dreadful condition because the weather was so hot and the plastic bags destroyed them. He had no respect for her whatsoever as far as I'm concerned and I didn't want him to think he could get off that easily by not having to tell the true story of what really happened that night.'

Peter wanted to know everything there was to know about how Kennedy killed his daughter, no matter how much he would be hurt by it. He knew that, during the struggle, Sheola had hit her head off something—possibly a lamppost—and that there were tears in the plastic bags which implied that Kennedy had dragged her from one place to another. Peter went to the Garda Ombudsman and told him that he wanted to know everything, medical and otherwise, about Sheola's death. And, eventually, he was allowed to go to his local garda station where he was shown all the documentation.

'The problem I have now is that what I was shown was the first Book of Evidence—there were two—and it never got to court. Because Kennedy changed his plea to guilty, none of what he said in the first Book of Evidence was brought up in the courtroom. In my mind, that means he got off lightly. And that breaks my heart, because I feel that Sheola deserves the full and true story to come out. I don't believe for one minute that she had consensual sex with Kennedy. I just do not believe it. And it really kills me that he could make out that she did. No forensic evidence to say she was even in his house that night ever came out in court.

'I wish the first Book of Evidence had been admissible and then the whole world would have known what really happened that night. I have had to accept how things went and be grateful that he would, one way or another, serve time for what he did and that I had a grave to go to where I could talk to my little girl.'

The last thing Peter ever wanted to do was to bury his daughter, but Kennedy's actions meant he had to endure the worst possible experience for any parent.

Peter also finds Kennedy's actions when Sheola was missing hard to accept. 'He walked around with us searching for her body for days and although I knew it was him from the very minute she went missing, he never let his guard down and he carried on with the whole act. People were coming up to him offering their sympathy and he accepted it, knowing he had done it. It's sick. But no matter how many times I go over it in my head, I know I can't turn back time.'

On 6 December 2006, Thomas Kennedy was sentenced to life imprisonment for the murder of Sheola Keaney. He did not speak when he was sentenced and his lawyers said nothing on his behalf.

Peter and Carol were allowed to make a Victim Impact Statement in court that day and Peter told those gathered that he couldn't describe in words the heartache and pain that he had been suffering since Sheola's death. 'To lose a child through illness or an accident is heartbreaking, but to lose a child in the way I did, with her basic right to life cruelly and unjustly taken away from her, has left me devastated.'

Carol spoke directly to her daughter from the witness box at the Central Criminal Court sitting. 'I sometimes dream that I get to the place where you died just in time to save you, then I wake up to realise you are gone. I dread to think how you suffered, I try to block it out, you poor child.'

Both parents were clearly devastated by the loss of their only child. And Peter says life hasn't got any easier.

'I think the hardest part for me was the first year. I can truthfully say that I was numb, literally numb and basically my concentration was nil and I couldn't work. I was very depressed. In fact, I only keep going nowadays with counselling, medication and friends. The hardest part for me is when I am alone with my thoughts. And it hurts me so much when I look at her stuff around the place and know that she's never going to be here again.

'The past 12 months have been quite tough. The numbness is wearing off and reality is setting in. I now know for a fact that I'm not going to get a phone call from her, or a text message, and I just find it upsetting to have to go to her grave. I keep telling myself in my head that she's not there, she's definitely not there, just to make myself feel that little bit better, but she is there. It's very hard to comprehend, because I now know that I'll never walk her down the aisle on her wedding day, I'll never see her get her degree from college.

'I see her friends and I know they are heartbroken over her, but they are able to move on and maybe travel over to America with their college degrees, and that hurts. I wanted Sheola to see the world and do well in life and that will never happen now.'

Peter finds Christmas and Sheola's birthday hard to cope with. He finds it hard to accept the way she died and thinks that if she had died in some other way, there'd be a reason for it, but he cannot understand how she could have been murdered, no matter how hard he tries. He'll never understand how anyone could have done what they did to his daughter.

He doesn't want Sheola to become another murder statistic. He believes that if her story will give even one man or woman the courage to walk away from an abusive relationship, then at least her death won't have been in vain.

'I hope that what happened to my child will send warning signs out to other families, and if they see similar traits in a relationship between their sons or daughters and a partner, I hope that they will jump in and do something about it. Try to advise the person to get out before it's too late. I was lucky enough that Sheola and I had a very good relationship; that we could actually tell each other bits and pieces. She was more like a friend than a daughter to me and being an only child we had a lot to discuss. And she was always very frank and open about Tom to me. I used to think that because she told me everything that nothing would happen because he would have been afraid of what I may have done to him if he had harmed Sheola. But I was very wrong. I think parents should just watch out for the warning signs when a relationship is in trouble.' Peter has been to a few meetings in Dublin with ADVIC (a support group for families of homicide victims) and sat with people who, like him, had lost a son or a daughter through murder. He says that that meeting was the first time in a long while that he felt normal. Knowing that there were other people going through the same grief and pain that he was going through helped him understand his feelings and put some perspective on what was happening. 'It did me good to know that I wasn't going mad,' he says. 'I was feeling exactly like all these other parents and there was nothing wrong with me.'

The group helped Peter to talk about his feelings towards Kennedy who, Peter feels, by saying Sheola had had consensual sex with him that day, had made it seem as if she was a 'cheap whore'.

'My daughter was far from cheap, she was classy. I never will believe that Sheola agreed to have sex with him. Until the day I die, I will swear blind that she did not allow him to have sex with her. Their relationship was over and she wanted it left that way. She was scared of him and she wanted nothing to do with him. She was just talking to him because she wanted to keep the peace. She didn't want to set him off. It was a comfort for me to talk to these people who had gone through similar experiences whereby the accused pleaded guilty and all the truth of what happened went out the window in a flash. They knew how I felt and it was a comfort to know that I wasn't the only one out there feeling so much anger over what had happened in court.'

Peter thinks the courts favour the offender. He also thinks the death penalty should be brought back for certain cases—like his daughter's—where a life has been taken. 'Take a life for a life,' he says. He doesn't understand why murderers should be allowed live, to be released from prison and walk the streets again, when they have taken an innocent person's life and destroyed a family. 'I think we should look at some sort of serious sentence,' he continues, 'not just letting them walk out the prison gate after seven or eight years, as happens in some cases.'

However, Peter is full of praise for the gardaí. 'In relation to the court case, the gardaí were great,' he says. 'They tried to explain everything to us right the way through.'

———

Peter remembers very clearly the first time he returned to Clonmel after Sheola's murder. He went to the local swimming pool and when he went into the sauna, everyone went quiet. To help the situation, he made a trivial comment about the day being a beautiful one and the atmosphere changed. He says the others there started to feel comfortable and relaxed around him.

He feels fortunate to have very good friends in Clonmel who know that if he's having a bad day, they should leave him alone and that if he's having a good day, they can chat away to him. He says they know the signs themselves, so they give him the privacy he needs. He still finds it hard to sit down and talk to someone about his daughter and he feels this is why more support is needed for people who have lost loved ones through murder. 'It's different to any other death and it needs to be dealt with differently,' he says. 'You can go to counselling and sit with people in a group who may have lost a mother, father or an aunt but they haven't lost them through murder, so they don't understand what you are going through. In fact if I was to sit with them, they would probably be traumatised by the time I'd have told Sheola's story. What we have gone through is totally different to other losses. And people just don't know how to deal with you.'

Peter has found it very difficult to move on. He takes one day at a time.

He finds mornings the worst and doesn't settle until his medication has started to work. Then he feels able to think clearly about the day. He also chain-smokes day and night, but tries to keep things in his life as normal as possible. He tries not to spend too much time lying in bed, even though, most times, that is all he feels like doing, he tries to get up early and have things to do— sorting the garden, meeting friends, maybe going down to the local pub and doing the crosswords. He tries not to shut himself off. He doesn't have much interest in starting new relationships because he finds it too difficult to go through everything again. 'At the moment I'm still raw,' he says, 'but I hope some day to wake up and feel that I can move on. There will always be difficulties though. A niece of mine had a baby recently and another niece had a christening and I forced myself to go to these things because you have no push in you at all. I always think of Sheola at these family occasions and they are hard days to get through, but no one can understand how hard it is to move on. Some days you're grand and other days it's just extremely hard, but you have to keep pushing yourself even though at times you just ask yourself, What's it all for?'

Peter says that one way to describe how he feels is that it is as if time has stopped for him. 'Maybe it's just my way of dealing with things,' he says, 'but there are just some things I can't change. Sheola had two bedrooms, her baby bedroom and her grown-up bedroom as she called it. Her computer is still there in her grown-up room. There's loads of photographs and a lot of memorabilia that she would have had from school. It's painted in lilac because she loved that colour and it's a real girl's room. When she died, I asked some of her friends to come up and pick something out that meant something to them, as a memory of Sheola, and one of the girls came up to me with a small photograph of three trees and she just burst out crying and she said that the picture symbolised the three girls, Sheola was the tall tree, Mary, the girl herself, was the middle tree and Laura, another pal, was the other tree. To anyone else it simply looked like a picture of a few trees, but to them it meant a lot.

'It breaks my heart when I look into her room that was once full of life and noise and laughter and hear nothing—it's basically dead. There was always music blaring from the room and I was always shouting up the stairs, "Turn it down." The house phone would be ringing non-stop and it was always for Sheola. I miss all that. I miss her company and having her friends running around the place. When I sit here at night now on my own, it's very hard. And I don't cope very well. If I could just turn back time I would, but it's out of my hands and I just have to accept that my beautiful daughter is gone forever.'

Peter feels closer to his daughter when he goes into her room, as if she is all around him. Though he does feel she is with him all the time. In the morning when he wakes, he sees her in his mind, laughing, and her face is the last image in his mind before he goes to sleep.

———

Stephen Rogers, a journalist with the *Irish Examiner*, covered Sheola's case. He remembers that the cathedral in Cobh was full as people came to pay their last respects to the family of a young girl who was only starting out on her life's journey with so much to live for.

'People go missing all the time around the country so when we heard a 19-year-old girl was missing no one really paid that much attention to it, because you always think that she could have just gone somewhere with her friends,' says Stephen. 'So, you don't actually react straight away. It was only when we got a call from one of our garda contacts who told us that there was something strange about this particular missing person's case that we sat up and took notice.'

He remembers that people were getting very concerned by the Saturday afternoon after Sheola hadn't turned up for work and that, by the Sunday, when gardaí had found her bag and shoes, everyone realised that something was very wrong. It was four hours after her bag had been found that gardaí recovered Sheola's body. Stephen remembered thinking of the case of 11-year-old Robert Houlihan whose body had been found near Cobh. The search for Robert had continued for days so, in comparison, Sheola's body was found quickly.

'Sheola had only been in Cobh for two years and yet she had built up a big group of friends, as well as maintaining the friends she had in Clonmel. As the search continued for her, people were coming up to us and talking about what a bubbly character she was, how well regarded she was, how she stood out from the crowd, not just because she was six foot tall but also because she had such an outgoing personality, a vivacious personality. When we heard all this, we knew that she wouldn't have been the type of girl to just disappear. She had so many friends and was obviously very well liked.

'Gardaí never once said publicly who they suspected of her killing, but the nature of the way she was found—with her shoes removed, her bag removed and a lot of her clothing removed—rumours were rife that she was either attacked by someone known to her who had flipped, or that it was just a random attacker.'

Within 24 hours of the forensic evidence being removed, gardaí had upgraded their investigation to a murder inquiry. Having contacted her friends and family, they identified Thomas Kennedy as Sheola's ex-partner. Gardaí questioned people about what sort of a relationship the two had had and, by the time of her funeral four or five days later, they seemed to have a very clear picture of what had happened and knew who their main suspect was.

'On the day of Sheola's removal, there must have been 500 or 600 people passing through the funeral home,' Stephen remembers. 'A large number of people had come from Clonmel, including Sheola's headmaster from Rockwell. He told me that he had to ring some of her friends in America to break the news and they were in an awful state and wondering if they should come home. They had finished school and had gone off to enjoy themselves. So it was a deeply depressed community in Clonmel.' Because of the number of people expected to attend Sheola's removal, there was a large garda presence for the occaision. Cobh came to a standstill during the removal and funeral. As Sheola's coffin passed through the streets on the way to the cathedral, people politely and respectfully lined the streets, bowed their heads and blessed themselves.'

The day of the funeral was very emotional for everybody. Two of Sheola's friends spoke from the altar, but they were barely able to contain their emotion. Both Sheola's mother and father had to be comforted by family and friends. At the end of the mass, the bishop, John McGee, made an address from the pulpit condemning what had happened and calling for the person responsible to come forward and give himself up.

The bishop is known for having a very direct approach in these sorts of situations and speaks directly to the murderer in each case. He knows that whatever he says will be publicised and that the person responsible will probably hear what he has said.

Stephen Rogers remembers that, on the day of the funeral, there were suspicions and rumours that someone was going to be arrested and it was probably going to be Thomas Kennedy. 'So the following day, I went to Cobh Garda Station at about 6 a.m. Shortly after I arrived, a number of gardaí left the station at high speed and went to Thomas Kennedy's address, arrested him and had him back at the station within an hour. They then proceeded to question him for most of that day. His father arrived at the scene shortly after his arrest and remained with him. He also arranged for legal representation for his son. On that Friday evening, Thomas Kennedy was brought to Middleton Garda Station and charged with Sheola Keaney's murder. Initially, the gardaí gave evidence in court to say that, when charged, Kennedy had said something along the lines of, "Plead guilty, I suppose." However, when the case finally came to trial he had changed his plea to not guilty.'

Kennedy gave evidence that he had had sex with Sheola the morning she was killed and that they had left his house together. He said that, as they had walked together, he had put an arm around her throat but that she had fallen to the ground—he didn't know what happened and when he realised she was dead, he panicked. He concealed her body and then went back and got the plastic bags in which gardaí would eventually find her wrapped.

However, the evidence showed that what had killed Sheola seemed to be more than just an accidental arm around her throat. She had been strangled. Marks were also found on her body that seemed to be consistent with the murderer kneeling on her chest whilst he was strangling her. Kennedy was told that this evidence would be heard in court. A week after the trial began, Kennedy suddenly changed his plea to guilty and, as a result, the judge had no choice but to impose a mandatory life sentence.

Sheola's murder shocked the town of Cobh and people there were sickened when they realised it was a man living within their own community who had killed her. 'It shook the whole area,' says Stephen Rogers. 'It was one of those murders that affected so many people.'

Some of Sheola's friends wrote a poem to her and, on the day of her burial, one of the girls stood and tearfully read the verses aloud. Everyone gathered in the packed cathedral heard how loving and special their dear friend had been to them.

'The Unforgettable Mark'
Friends come and go like the changing of seasons

Summer through autumn, winter through spring
Friends they are plenty and easy to find
Unlike Sheola who was one of a kind
They don't come round often, but you were magical to find
You were there for us, cared for us and made each and every
one of us smile
True friends stick by you through thick and through thin
Never judge you or betray you and always love what's within
Provide a shoulder, a hand, a loving heart
For that Sheola you will leave an unforgettable mark.

———

The Keaney family felt lucky to have been able to say a few words about their beloved daughter in court. However, many other families who have lost children through murder or manslaughter have not been afforded the same right and this has had a profound effect on those left behind.

Joan Dean, the founder of ADVIC, a support group for families affected by murder or homicide, believes that the Irish legal system has a long way to go before life becomes a little easier for the families of victims. For example, she feels that families are deeply upset about the fact that they have no given right to make a Victim Impact Statement—it is an issue that ADVIC is trying to change.

The group was founded by a number of families who had been bereaved by murder but that the group now also represents families bereaved by homicide. The term 'homicide' is used because many members of the group would have had a verdict other than murder. 'The verdict may have been for manslaughter, wrongful death, unlawful killing, a lot of these ridiculous labels that the law puts on the killing of a human being,' says Joan, 'and we felt that if we used 'murder', the term might make some people feel excluded because they didn't have a murder verdict. To date, we've helped in excess of 160 families, but we have just under 100 families on our database because some families who contact us may not be ready to join, they may feel they need more time to accept things. Every second year, we have a memorial service for victims of homicide and, last year, it was held in St Anne's Church in Dawson Street, Dublin, and over 450 people attended. That gives us an idea of the scale of the impact of murder.'

Alan Shatter's Victim's Right Bill came before the Dáil in mid-2008, but the government shut it down so that they would be able to bring in their own bill sometime in 2009. That this private member's bill was not acted upon angers Joan. 'As it stood before the House, it could have been approved and taken to the next stage where amendments could have been added and the government could have then had its own input. It would have meant that victims would have rights, in legislation, within months.'

There were many facets to Shatter's bill but it would have given the families of homicide victims rights in legislation, which they don't have at the moment. Today the system doesn't recognise family members of a homicide victim as victims themselves, so they have no place in the system.

Joan says that if Shatter's bill had been passed, it would have automatically afforded rights to the victim. It would have given families the right to information. At the moment, a family has to go and seek out the information themselves, which can be difficult. Information is not offered to them.

'We would have had the right to give a Victim Impact Statement in all cases,' says Joan. 'At present, that's not the case. That's a very, very important thing for families after a homicide. At present, a family has no right to give a Victim Impact Statement in the case of a murder verdict. It is at the discretion of the judge. There is some legislation there for a manslaughter verdict, but, again, it's at the discretion of the judge, and we know from some recent high-profile cases that it doesn't happen and it causes a huge concern to families. I think in terms of being able to take the stand, families have a need to portray their loved one as a human being, not just a dead person with injuries. And they should be awarded that right. It's the least they can do for families who have lost someone they love so brutally.'

But Joan knows that she has a lot of work to do to convince some legal representatives who have serious objections to her aims being achieved. One of the objections made is that if a person is articulate or well read, they can present a more powerful impact statement, as opposed to somebody who may have difficulty speaking in public, or who may have literacy issues. ADVIC's argument to this is that there are accused people going to court every single day who have problems with literacy and who may not be articulate, but they are afforded any legal support required and assistance with their court case. It argues that the same legal help and assistance should be afforded to victims.

'The department of justice has promised that it will give victim status to the families of homicide victims,' says Joan. 'That would be a huge step forward for us, because then the legal profession would have to treat victims' families with respect and they would also have to protect their rights. Politicians are a whole other story. There have been cases where politicians have written to the prison service and the parole board, looking for early release for prisoners or to have prisoners transferred for some reason or another. It seems our entire system is weighted very heavily in favour of the offender and maybe that's one of the reasons why society has become more violent. I don't think it's the main reason, but we give out a very soft message when we don't apply the law, when we don't apply the sentencing and we don't insist that sentences are served in full. And it's definitely a part of the problem.'

As a group, ADVIC feels that 25 years would be an appropriate sentence for taking a life and that the review for parole shouldn't happen before the person responsible has served 15 years of his/her sentence. At the moment, somebody serving a life sentence can come up for parole after seven years and, theoretically, could be released at that point.

Joan says another worry families have is in relation to the trial. When somebody pleads guilty to murder, the trial does not go ahead, therefore the family rarely finds out all the details of what happened. In other countries, such as France, where they have a Civil Law System, a trial may still go ahead if it is felt to be in the interest of the victim. ADVIC believes Ireland should operate the same system. 'I don't see why elements of best practice in other countries can't be brought into our own system. It is very important for families to know exactly what happened to their loved ones, even if they know what they may hear may hurt them even more. But they should have the right to know everything when a family member is killed. I think a final conviction is very important. I don't feel the word 'closure' is the right word to use, although it is used very often. The final conviction brings an end to that particular journey, but the hole that's left in your life is never filled, and can never be filled. You never get over it and time doesn't heal it. You just find a way to live with it, cope with it and you try to stop yourself being identified by it. But life will never be the same again.'

———

Margaret Martin, Director of Women's Aid, is becoming increasingly worried about the dramatic rise in the murder rate of Irish women that has occurred over the past few years. She sees women every day who live in fear of their partners and worry about their safety, and in a lot of cases the safety of their children too. She advises anyone in an abusive relationship to seek help and start planning their escape as soon as the warning signs appear.

'There have been 140 women murdered since 1996 and, of those, the majority of them—roughly 90 per cent—have been murdered by someone they know,' she says. 'About half of these women have been murdered by a partner or ex-partner and almost two thirds have been murdered in their own homes. 'That's the type of pattern that we have seen emerge over the past ten years or so here in Ireland.

International research shows similar trends. A study of 11 cities in the United States showed that out of 220 homicides and attempted homicides, 70 per cent of the women attacked had already been physically abused by the partner who attacked them, giving a very clear connection between homicide and domestic violence.

'There are a number of things that have developed over the last few years that have been identified as 'risk indicators', the things in a relationship that could affect a woman's risk of being attacked, or even murdered,' Margaret says. 'For example, if there's a potential or actual separation, then the woman is at a higher risk of being assaulted. People often ask, "Well if she's being abused, why doesn't she leave?" but they don't realise that sometimes by leaving it can actually heighten the risk factor for her.'

In 2005, the National Crime Council undertook research which found that a third of the people who were being abused and who had left the relationship to escape, continued to be victims of abuse in one way or another. Leaving the abusive relationship does not always guarantee that the abuse will stop. However, if a woman seeks proper support and proper information before leaving, it can work. Margaret says that it is important for women to know that, done properly and with help from the right channels, two thirds of women who choose to leave their perpetrator will be safe.

'If someone is in an abusive relationship, the first step is to call somewhere like Women's Aid. There is a system of safety planning in operation there and the staff will talk you through it and help in whatever way they can so that, when the time is right for that woman to leave her home, she has people around her who can assist her. But a woman who is in a situation like this also needs to look at the legal repercussions before they do anything rash. For example, most women might feel that they would be automatically entitled to a barring order from the courts, but that's not always the case. They don't just automatically hand out barring orders in court, so it's important to sit down with a solicitor or somebody in the legal profession and see what options are best for your own personal situation.

'The woman herself will know the type of reaction she will get if she does pack up and go, so it's important that she plans well in advance if she is thinking of leaving. She needs to have a safe place to go so that she does not put herself in even more danger than before. For example, in Dublin there are a number of women's refuges but, unfortunately, there are not always places available. If needed, the women can be put up in a bed and breakfast accommodation or a regular hostel temporarily but her safety should always be her first concern. A B&B might not be the safest of places, depending on the type of person you are trying to escape from.

'Each relationship is different and each woman knows the potential of her partner to cause her harm, so she has to plan meticulously so that she, and in some cases her children, are as safe as possible and out of immediate danger.'

In the United States, psychologist David Adams interviewed 31 men who had been convicted of murdering their partners and, from those interviews, he was able to identify five different types of abuser.

One of which was the 'materially motivated man'. This type of man murders out of fear that the status quo in his relationship is going to be threatened. For example, if a family lived in a really nice house, had a family business or a whole lifestyle that was dependent on your partner or you wife continuing to live with you, then that would be threatened by her leaving. So there is a particular group of men who murder simply because of the fear that their lives as they know it will be upset by their partner choosing to leave.

When people hear of a partner killing his wife or girlfriend, they often think that it was a 'crime of passion', that the man just lost control at that time, when his passions were running high, and they killed. But through his research, Adams identified men who fitted into the 'jealous type and of those he identified in the US, half had been convicted of first degree murder, which means there was premeditation.

This research shows that these men had not murdered their partners in a 'crime of passion' but that they were very much calculated, premeditated killings. These men would have possibly stalked their partner, would have known her movements. They could have been tracking her for days, maybe weeks, and they would often be carrying a weapon so that when the opportunity arose they could then kill.

Margaret Martin thinks the problem with the term 'crime of passion' is that it can portray the murderer as a victim of his emotions, of his passion, suggesting that the murder was something that was outside his control. This is something that he can then use to elicit a certain level of sympathy, particularly from a jury, during a trial. 'You hear people say, "He loved her too much", but how can that be possible, you cannot measure love,' she says. 'There is no place for violence in love. Love and violence don't sit together. There might be obsession or desire, the murder may have issues about wanting to own somebody, to control them, but it's not love in any intimate way, in any caring way. And it's really important that when we hear those kinds of thing that we start to challenge them and not accept them as being an acceptable way to talk about something as serious as murder or physical assault of attempted homicide.'

Margaret says that a lot of women talk to friends and to family, but Irish research has shown that a third of people who are abused never tell anyone. She feels this is a huge burden for a woman to carry by herself. She feels it is important to understand that domestic violence is not a one-off event, but that it forms a pattern. It may take a woman some time to realise that what is happening may not be simply be because her attacker was under a lot of pressure in some part of his life, such as his job. 'There may be one act and then another, a couple of weeks later, they could be spread out. And, in these cases, it can take a while for the woman to accept that this man's actions are not being caused by a stressful day at work.

'It can take a while for a woman who has been abused to talk,' she says. 'And, when they do, research has shown that some of these women have been assaulted 35 times or more before they approached the police. That shows how, a lot of the time, women watch and wait, take the abuse and hang on to see if it happens again or if it's just a one-off. But it can be very hard, especially at the start of a relationship, for a woman to tell someone else that she is concerned about her partner's behaviour, even to friends. This is because a woman may not want her friends to think she is bad mouthing her partner or she may not want people to think that she made a wrong decision in getting involved with this particular man.

'Sometimes, particularly if she is young, a woman might be worried about people telling her, "I told you so." Something that can happen easily if she is involved with a man her family doesn't like. So there mightn't be a lot of space for her to be able to talk about it.'

In Ireland, Domestic Violence Legislation comes into force when a person reaches 18 years of age, so it doesn't protect younger women. Margaret thinks more initiatives, targeted at particularly young women and young men, are needed as dating abuse and dating violence is increasing in Ireland. She doesn't feel enough is being done to tackle this at an early stage or, more importantly, to stop it from happening in the first place. This issue should be discussed in secondary schools so that young people have an understanding of what can happen to them and also of what is right and what is wrong in a dating relationship. 'Young people should be educated in relationships and what the boundaries are from their teenage years,' she says. 'That is the only way we can try and combat this issue before it spirals out of control.'

Another area of domestic violence that tends to shock people is that of abuse towards pregnant women. A quarter of women who suffer physical abuse at the hands of a partner start being abused when they are pregnant. 'This can be a very hard situation to cope with for any woman because she may feel trapped in the relationship knowing that she is about to have a baby with this person,' Margaret says. 'But a woman should never allow herself to stay in that situation simply because she is pregnant. Her safety and the safety of her unborn child have to be the priority. And she has to seek help as soon as the abuse starts.'

Although Women's Aid is getting more calls from people who are experiencing abuse at the hands of a partner, it is hard to say whether or not domestic violence is on the increase. There are many women out there who stay in a relationship for one reason or another and say nothing.

In the UK, Baroness Scotland, the attorney general, was speaking recently about the Greater London Area, where a whole series of integrated measures had been brought in to combat domestic violence. With these measures in place, over a four-year period, the number of domestic violence murders went from 32 to just four. So prevention can sometimes be the cure. Margaret Martin feels it is important that the Irish learn from others and 'piggy back' on these lessons to change things in Ireland.

'Sometimes people assume that domestic violence only occurs in certain classes or within certain ethnic groups, but all this demonstrates is that money can enable people to be much more private. A woman with no money will seek help and will be dependent on the state to survive, so her case will become much more public than that of a woman who has financial stability and could leave of her own free will and support herself financially. A woman like this may never have to tell anyone about her situation, if she is able to survive alone.

'Domestic violence takes many forms and many women experience all of those forms. The one that's most commonly disclosed to us on the helpline is emotional abuse. The level of threat that a woman might be living with may be really extreme, which can sometimes be hard for people to understand. So while a woman may never be physically abused, she may be living with the threat that she is going to be abused. One threat that we hear about from women, and it's something that is quite worrying, is that a partner threatens to take the kids, get them into the car and crash it, killing himself and the kids. So, it may not be a direct threat to her, it may be to people she loves or it may be to himself.

'Abusers tend to try and wear their partner down through mental abuse by continually telling them they are stupid, fat or a bitch, and this can be very hard to live with. Being continually abused like this has a corrosive effect, and over a long period of time that is what does the damage. Very often women say to us that they find that much more difficult to deal with and much more hurtful. But this in no way undermines the physical abuse that women in Ireland are experiencing, but I think very often people are surprised at just how extreme that verbal abuse can be.'

Those, like Margaret Martin, at Women's Aid are hearing more stories of abuse, of women who are regularly being strangled and choked into unconsciousness, being very badly physically abused, being dragged around by the hair, being head-butted, being attacked with all kinds of common household items—golf clubs, tools, all sorts of different things. They are also hearing about more women who are experiencing financial abuse, where their partner goes through the bin, for example, checking to see if there are things there that he wouldn't consider to be waste. He may also go through every item on a bill, making sure that it all adds up, and then will tell his partner/wife that she is not allowed spend money on personal items, even that she can't buy certain items of food.

'The woman in this situation may have very little money,' Margaret says, 'and so things that other people take for granted, like meeting a friend for a coffee, can't be done because the woman is too embarrassed to say she has no money and that, in turn, means that she has no escape from the house because she has no money to spend.'

Recently, Women's Aid has also become concerned about the level of sexual abuse that is being reported. 'We know from research that was done in Ireland that 25 per cent of sexual abuse is perpetrated by intimate partners. The level of sexual abuse that's even disclosed to us is quite low, at around 10 per cent, because women find it so extremely difficult to talk about because, in some cases, these women are not only being raped but then further degraded by being urinated on. And it can be very difficult to even talk about that. And a lot of women are being raped shortly after childbirth or when they are heavily pregnant and it's very distressing to even admit to someone that this is happening to you.'

Margaret's advice to any woman who finds herself in an abusive relationship is to call Women's Aid and speak in confidence to someone there. She knows that that phone call can make a world of a difference to someone who is being abused and who feels there is no one they can confide in because of the embarrassment they feel.

'There is an assumption that if you're in a relationship with someone you are constantly sexually available to them and that's not right,' she says. 'We've gone from a country with a big history of not talking about sex to talking about sex very freely. But talking about negative sexual experiences can be very difficult but it's something that we need to discuss and it needs to be brought out into the open. Domestic violence because of its very nature, is hidden, it's a secret, it's not talked about and it's important as a nation that we change that.'

07 | FAMILICIDE

THE DUNNE FAMILY

On a wet Monday afternoon, 23 April 2007, the bodies of Adrian Dunne (29), his wife, Ciara (26), and their two little daughters, Lean (five) and Shania (three), were found at their family home in Moin Rua Estate in Monageer, just outside Clonroche, County Wexford.

Gardaí had forced their way into the little white bungalow after concerns were raised for the safety of the family who had not been seen over the weekend. Despite these concerns and the gardaí's suspicions that something may have happened at the house, none of the officers were prepared for the sickening scene that confronted them. As one garda looked through the letterbox he saw a man's body hanging in the hallway.

Adrian was found hanging from a ligature fastened to a roof rafter. He was wearing a Glasgow Celtic jersey and jeans. His wife lay slumped on the floor, strangled, with a ligature around her neck, and the bodies of their two little daughters lay propped up on pillows on the sofa in the cosy sitting room—the pretty little girls appeared to have been suffocated with the very pillows on which they lay. They were lying toe to toe covered by a duvet. Both were dressed in pyjamas and each held a Dora the Explorer soft doll. A medical examination showed that Ciara had bruising under her scalp and may have been rendered concussed before being strangled. She showed no signs of a struggle. Adrian finally completed the plan by hanging himself in the hallway. Two mobile phones were taken away from the house for forensic examination. Sexually explicit text messages were found stored on a pink Nokia phone. A silver Nokia held an eerie text in the outbox that stated: 'Please ring father x from Wexford and tel him Ciara and Adrian are so very sorry. We nott going to Livepol. Instad we pick heaven ... Please for give.' The text had been sent but never received by the recipient, Beat 102/103, a radio station based in Waterford.

All four had died in what is now loosely termed in Ireland familicide—the taking of the lives of a whole family by a parent, before that parent finally kills him or her self.

The country was sickened to hear how the two little girls had been so callously murdered when their lives were only just beginning and neighbours in the quiet area were shocked when they heard of the horrific discovery in their little horseshoe estate.

But, in reality, few people there really knew the quiet, introverted couple, who, for some reason, chose to keep themselves to themselves and never really mixed with their neighbours. Adrian's mother, Mary, agrees with this. 'They weren't a couple to mix. But I lived in Ferns for seven years and I didn't know my next-door neighbour. I never bothered. The children knew the other children all right but myself and Hugh we didn't bother with anyone. We kept ourselves to ourselves, we didn't bother mixing with anyone. We knew people when we went out all right, we were playing music so we were going out into the public eye, so we had to mix with people and be friendly—and people were friendly with us. There were the odd few all right that would pass a remark about us having problems with our sight, but you meet that no matter what.'

Adrian was blind. He had had no sight in one eye from birth and had lost his sight in his second eye after an illness when he was seven. His wife, Ciara, originally from County Donegal, had no problems with her vision but, unfortunately, for this apparently loving couple, their two little girls had inherited the visual impairment of their father's family, congenital cataracts, and both were losing their sight rapidly with the likelihood of becoming totally blind.

This may be the reason why their parents didn't let them mix too much with other children and never allowed anyone other than themselves or close family to mind them. Maybe they felt their children would be teased by others of the same age because of their disability. No one will ever know.

But locals in Monageer often gossiped about the family and struggled to understand why they were so distant from everyone else in the tight-knit community.

As the details surrounding the tragedy were uncovered, the biggest shock came a few days after the discovery of the bodies when a local funeral director confirmed that Adrian, Ciara and the children had all visited her office shortly before they died. The family did not want to enquire about the price of plots in the local graveyard or to organise their own funeral costs should anything ever happen to them, they had, in fact, called to the funeral director to discuss and plan a funeral service for themselves and their two little girls.

Adrian even went as far as to tell the funeral director that they wished the children be buried in their Dora jeans, should they die before the age of six in some sort of accident. Ciara enquired about little white and pink coffins for her two little angels, an unusual request at the best of times. The funeral director was so shocked and uncomfortable about the meeting that she phoned the gardaí to let them know what had happened.

However, despite the concerns of the undertaker and the action of the gardaí to alert the social services department of the local HSE, social workers did not visit the family over the coming days. The department later stated that its staff do not work outside of office hours—an issue that has been raised in the Wexford area a number of times before, following other tragic suicides within the community.

Compounding the tragedy was the fact that no one thought of speaking to the extended Dunne family, who lived only a short drive away, about what had happened and no one thought of calling to Adrian's mother to tell her about their worries. Bizarrely, local gardaí decided not to call to the Dunne house that weekend, choosing instead to drive by the home to see if they noticed anything unusual.

———

On the morning of 5 April 2007, Adrian Dunne, Ciara and the girls arrived by appointment at a solicitor's office in Enniscorthy to make a will. Instructions were given that if Adrian died first his wife was to inherit from him and in the event of both deaths their children were to be the benefactors. If Ciara was to die first her wishes mirrored her husband's. Adrian said one reason he wanted to make a will was because a brother of his had committed suicide. They stipulated that they did not wish for either of their families to take care of the children in the event of their deaths as they did not have a good relationship with them. According to the Monageer Report which looked at the circumstances surrounding and prior to their deaths, the family appeared to be very happy.

It was a lovely sunny Friday morning on 20 April 2007 when Adrian and Ciara packed their daughters into their silver Opel Corsa to head into New Ross, County Wexford. Adrian had rung the funeral parlour earlier in the week to make an appointment, so they drove first to a local health centre and on to the undertakers. The young dad was eager to make funeral plans for his family and Ciara appeared to go along with the idea.

The Dunne family arrived at the funeral parlour at 2 p.m. The funeral director welcomed them into the office and was obviously surprised that Adrian and Ciara were so concerned about their funeral plans. The couple took a seat on the red leather sofa as the children played around them. They appeared to be very relaxed, were casually dressed and made the usual small talk before addressing the purpose of their visit—options for their burial.

Despite their young age, and the age of the children, Adrian and Ciara insisted that they wanted everything in place, in case they all died in a car crash or had an accident of some sort, as they said they were planning a trip away to watch a Liverpool game. Adrian was a huge fan of the club and had been to Anfield a number of times. The couple said that if they all died when the children were under the age of six, they wanted one child to be buried with each parent, Adrian with Lean and Shania with Ciara. If the children were older, they wanted a pink and white coffin for each of them. When the funeral director asked what would happen if the children were to grow up and get married, Ciara replied that this would never happen.

They also outlined how they wanted the children to wear their Liverpool jerseys and their Dora jeans when they were buried, as she was their favourite cartoon character. Adrian was to be buried wearing his treasured football jersey. He also wanted 'You'll Never Walk Alone' and Led Zeppelin's 'Stairway to Heaven' sung at the church. Father Richard Redmond, a friend of the Dunnes, was to officiate over the mass and all of the family were to be buried together in the cemetery in Boolavogue, where a heart-shaped headstone was to be placed on the grave.

The funeral director wrote everything down as they chatted, acting very normal, but her concern for the welfare of the children was growing by the minute. She had genuine concerns about the purpose of the visit and feared that the children were in acute danger. When she had said goodbye to the family, she phoned a local garda and told him about what had happened. He suggested a call to Fr Redmond, the priest Adrian had requested for the funeral mass. For the rest of the day, as she carried on her work, the funeral director prayed that nothing sinister would happen to the family in the meantime.

The Dunnes seemed happy with the visit and drove off in their car, back to their cosy little home where, unknown to Ciara and the girls, they were to spend their last few days on earth.

Mary Frances Ryan, a reporter at the time with *The Enniscorthy Echo*, covered the tragedy.

'We found out that, on the Friday morning, the family were visited by a public health nurse who had come to check on the

children's eye impairments. She told gardaí that she didn't
notice anything unusual. Then that afternoon the family went
down to New Ross to the undertakers. They visited a local shop on
the way and the children were playing around in the shop, as
children do. But when they got to Cooney's Undertakers, they
made specific enquiries and gave specific direction about how
they wanted their funeral to be. What was particularly eerie about
the instructions was that they specified what they wanted for the
children, if they were under six years of age when they died, or if
they were over six—giving details right down to what they should
wear in the coffins. It's not something that parents would normally
be thinking about, so alarm bells started to ring.'

Father Redmond rang Adrian Dunne on his mobile phone that
Friday evening. Adrian said they were visiting the family grave in
Boolavogue but that they would meet him at the house. Father
Redmond arrived there at 7 p.m. He told the inquiry team that
there seemed to be an air of excitement at the house and everyone
was happy. After about half an hour the priest broached the subject of the visit to the funeral director. Ciara Dunne got very irate
and asked if he thought they were going to hurt the children.
Adrian said it was simply in case they ever had a car accident. The
Dunnes told Father Redmond they were planning to move to
Liverpool and it all seemed plausible. When he left after about two
hours he felt somewhat relieved. The following morning the
curate rang Adrian's mobile but it was turned off. After the news
of the tragedy broke, Adrian's brother, Sebastian, said he had been
talking to his brother on the phone on Saturday and that everything seemed to be ok.

The gardaí have the power to take a child into care if they feel
that there is a danger to the child—but this never happened. A
patrol car is understood to have patrolled the estate over the weekend, once in the early hours of Sunday morning and then again in
the early hours of Monday morning at around 12.30 a.m., but no
one entered the house and spoke to the family. The gardaí saw the
curtains drawn and the car parked outside and assumed everything was fine—but things were far from fine. On Saturday at

1 p.m. the Garda Superintendent phoned the childcare manager and left a message on his mobile phone. When he called back he said he would follow up on the case, however the Monageer Report found that the childcare manager who would have had responsibility for the area said he was off duty that weekend, his mobile was off and he received no message from the other manager. Gardaí found evidence that a call had been made to that number. The first childcare manager advised the Garda Superintendent of the fact that there was no out-of-hours service but that the gardaí had the power to take the children from the home if he felt that they were at risk.

The Monageer Report found that the deaths may have occurred early on the Saturday morning. As the news gradually emerged of the sickening scene which lay inside the house, the sense of disbelief and shock hit everyone in the small estate. People could not believe what had happened.

Mary Frances remembers people arriving at their homes on the estate and, on hearing what had happened at the house, they put their faces in their hands and started to cry. Everyone was so overwhelmed with the shock about what they were being told had happened on their doorstep. The estate is very quiet and over the previous few days, children would have been out playing and people were totally distressed to think that a whole family could have been killed right beside them.

Initially, people spoke of the Dunnes as being a close-knit family, who were 'always together'. Neighbours said they were never seen on their own. But after a couple of days, people began to mention that Adrian appeared to be domineering, the stronger force in the family. Neighbours also said that if Ciara visited a neighbour for a cup of tea, the children would arrive shortly after and say that their daddy wanted her back in the house. 'They never went out on their own,' says Mary. 'Ciara didn't go on her own. Adrian didn't go on his own. They wouldn't even come up here on their own. I never knew Ciara or Adrian to be anywhere without the other.'

It also emerged that Adrian and Ciara had got married very quickly, in a surprise wedding that Adrian had planned himself.

Despite these comments, everyone continued to say how united the family seemed and how they appeared to enjoy doing things together. Everyone seemed to know that the family loved Liverpool and were planning a trip to watch a game in the coming months.

It later emerged that they had planned a permanent move to Liverpool but it had fallen through shortly before their deaths; it also emerged that everything wasn't particularly great with Ciara's family. It was said that Ciara's mother had tried to visit the family on a number of occasions without success and word from Donegal was that she had not been allowed to see her daughter or that it had been made difficult for her to see her daughter after Ciara went to live in Wexford.

There appeared to be tension below the surface for this apparently close-knit family.

————

Adrian Dunne first met Ciara O'Brien in Dublin when he was studying on a media course. He would spend the week in Dublin and go home to his family in Wexford at the weekends. His mother, Mary, has said that he seemed to be very happy with his life in Dublin and that he had hoped to get a career in radio eventually. His choice of work in that field, however, was seriously curtailed because of his blindness but he remained hopeful that he could break into the media at some stage.

'Adrian never let anything better him,' Mary says. 'If he wanted to do something, he did it. If he made up his mind he was going to do something, then he did it. He never let his sight get the better of him. God, I've seen him here for hours trying to write his name. And he got so that he'd be able to write his name for a bank or anything like that. And he got so that he was able to write his name as good as anyone who'd be able to see.'

Mary remembers the weekend when Adrian brought Ciara home to meet her and her husband, Hughie. They both thought she was lovely. Hughie and Ciara got on very well and Mary thought she was a 'very nice girl'. She says Adrian and Ciara seemed to get on 'like a house on fire', so she never interfered in their relationship, just as she never interfered in any of her children's relationships. All she cared about was that they were happy.

'You could see that the two of them were serious about each other,' she says. 'They were doing everything together from the very beginning. And she stuck up for Adrian from the very beginning and I will have to say she was a very good girl because she knew nothing about people being blind, but she was prepared to give him a chance and that was more important than anything, that she wasn't going to come down on him about his sight. And when Lean was born and her sight was affected, the same as Adrian's, Ciara didn't moan and groan about the fact that the child was blind. When she was pregnant the second time and little Shania was affected as well, she still coped with it. She hadn't any problem with looking after the three of them and she said that.

'She said they were hers and that's all she cared about, that was her life. And they were happy together, God rest them both.'

Adrian and Ciara had planned to get married three or four times before they actually did and they only told Adrian's family about a month before the ceremony. They had a small wedding in Bray on New Year's Eve, 2005, with only a few people present. The group then went to a local pub and had a few drinks, everyone enjoyed the day. But Ciara didn't invite her family, Mary doesn't think she even told them about it, but says that was her own decision and not Adrian's because Ciara made her own mind up. Mary doesn't think Ciara had much contact with her family, even at that stage.

After the family's death, the extent of the division between the two families became evident in the final funeral arrangements for the family. Adrian's wishes to have the family buried together in Boolavogue never came to pass, despite their efforts to ensure that their wishes were put down on paper. Ciara's family drove from Donegal and informed the Dunne family that they were taking Ciara and the little girls back with them to be buried in Gort. This distressed Adrian's family but they finally agreed to the request of

P.J. and Marian O'Brien. This meant that Adrian was buried in the local cemetery in Boolavogue—but without his beloved family. Some of his wishes were granted, though, and the songs he requested were played at his funeral.

————

It was an incredibly tragic and sad time for the Dunne family. Only a month previously Adrian's brother, James, had been buried in the same graveyard, and had had his funeral mass in the same church. He had committed suicide. It was heartbreaking for the family to have to go back to that same church in even more tragic circumstances.

Both families were understandably devastated by the events that unfolded that weekend. And both are angered by how little was done to protect all four of the family, despite all the warning signs.

Adrian's mother cannot understand why no one called to the family if they were so concerned about their well being. And despite a report from the Monageer Inquiry stating that Adrian strangled his wife and murdered his children, Mary struggles to believe that her son could do such a horrible thing to those he loved.

At the time the family died, there were rumours around the village that Adrian was in serious financial difficulty and that loan sharks were harassing him to repay a large loan. He had told his mother that he was struggling to make ends meet and even, at times, had resorted to gambling. Mary admits her son enjoyed placing a few bets on the horses but she refuses to believe that his financial difficulties contributed to his death and that of his wife and children.

'He had a financial debt,' she says, 'he owed money and sure with only getting social welfare you're not going to pay a whole lot back. By the time you provide for yourself and your family, you're not going to have an awful lot left to be able to pay back anything. And the pressures were on him for to pay back what he'd got. I don't believe anyone should go near moneylenders, I never have, they're serious people and I told him at the time not to do it. To be honest I don't know how much he owed. And I don't know whether he had gone more into gambling, or what it was that really brought up his debts. I know he used to go on holidays, but holidays wouldn't have brought it up that much. But no matter what he would have been doing Ciara would have known because she was with him all the time.

'Adrian did come to me looking for €50,000, but I said to him that I hadn't got it, I hadn't a hope in hell of having it. He said, "Well Mammy, I wanted it for yesterday rather than today" and I knew he was worried. I said, "Sure why don't you go to the guards and tell them you're worried about what might happen to you if you don't pay it back." And he said to me, "I can't go to the guards, Mammy, sure they've threatened Ciara and the children. They've threatened to kill me." I then said, "Well, sure, I'll go the guards for you then." But he said, "No, Mam. I don't want anything to happen to you either."

'The guards did ask me after this all happened if I knew any names of who the moneylenders were, but I don't and I don't want to know. And I said they're people I'd have nothing at all to do with. They're bad people. It was a stupid thing for him to do. Ciara knew about it because they were following her around as well, when she was going around in the car they were following her. She was pretty upset about it too.

'I think that it wasn't so much as they couldn't see a way forward, it was the fact that moneylenders are ruthless, we all know that. They don't mind what they do or what they don't do. They get their money one way or the other. I don't think it's so much what Ciara or Adrian done, it's what someone else done and I don't think there's anybody looking into that end and I don't believe there is going to be anyone looking into that either. I have tried to talk to the guards about this but they tried to fob me off by saying there was no one else involved. Maybe there was no one else involved, but to my dying day I won't believe it. Adrian loved his family. He lived for them. They were everything to him and he loved Ciara. They went everywhere together. And they lived for their two little girls. The media have made Adrian out of be some kind of monster, but he was not like that at all. They struggled to get by because Adrian wanted the best for them. He wanted a job. That's what had got poor Adrian into trouble in the first place. He had wanted to start up his own business so he borrowed, and he borrowed from the wrong people. And he ran into trouble and he wasn't able to pay back what he had borrowed. He was into wicker work, you know making baskets and stools and things like that, himself and his daddy used to do them and they'd go to a car boot sale down in New Ross.

'They used to go there every Sunday before Hughie died and sell their stuff off and go and buy more stuff and you see Adrian wanted to try and start up his own business making and selling wicker products. Ciara's family had what Adrian hadn't got, but he wanted to give Ciara what her family would have been able to give her, but he just wasn't able to. He was stupid to even try and compete with them.'

She remembers how he would take his family on holidays, just to let Ciara's family know that he could go on the same type of holiday as they went on. 'But they were no more alike than cheese is like chalk,' she says. 'It was as simple as that. He couldn't live up to the standards that he wanted to live up to. He was trying to make Ciara feel that she wasn't being left out of anything like that, that he could give her as much as they would have been able to give her.'

Even with the problems they faced, Mary believes that family was happy. The children were given everything they needed—a television, a video, a DVD—there was nothing that they didn't get. The family took holidays and the girls would take their toys with them. Adrian and Ciara spent any money they had on their daughters. 'They didn't spare any money on those children,' she says.

Mary insists that, despite reports to the contrary, Adrian wanted Ciara to maintain contact with her family in Donegal. She says that he encouraged her all the time to go back home for a break, but Ciara chose not to of her own free will. 'The papers made Adrian out to be a right bully boy altogether, saying he controlled Ciara. If you were to go by the papers, Adrian would have been an awful case altogether, but I didn't know the Adrian they printed about in the papers. I never seen that in Adrian and I never seen that in Ciara, because Ciara would take your life over Adrian. She wouldn't let you say a wrong word about him.'

Mary remembers reading an article and when she had finished she commented that it was a good job Ciara was dead because she'd have been up in arms about it. 'The media seemed to put Adrian down regardless. Maybe that's because he was a man, I don't know but they seemed to blame him. They put him down as being a murderer. But I don't put him down as being a murderer because I don't put anyone down. You can't judge a person unless you really know what happened. There was no one else there, the ones who were there are dead. And they're the only ones that would be able to give us the answers that we want. None of my family can sleep at night or rest thinking about the lads. There's no one here in this house who would blame Ciara or Adrian for what happened.'

Mary doesn't believe that she'll ever get all the answers she wants. She described the findings of the Monageer Report as a whitewash and refuses to accept that her son could have killed his family.

––––

The O'Brien family never accepted the marriage between their daughter and Adrian Dunne. In fact, there was little or no communication between the family from Donegal and their only child for nearly two years. Ciara had moved to Wexford with Adrian and, for some reason known only to herself, made the decision not to keep in touch with her mother and father. A priest who is a friend of the family had tried unsuccessfully to make contact with Ciara on a number of occasions. Some local people felt that Adrian controlled his young wife, a rumour his family are quick to deny.

Friends of the O'Briens say that the family was distraught at being cut out of their daughter's life and at not being able to see their grandchildren.

When the decision was made to bury Ciara and her daughters in Donegal, the Dunnes were obviously upset. However, they agreed to split up the family if the O'Briens agreed to all four of the family being waked in the Dunne house, so that they could be together as a family for one last time. Adrian, Ciara and their daughters were in closed coffins and neither family had a chance to say a last goodbye face to face with the ones they loved. It was heartbreaking for the Dunnes to see the family separated, but both families were in pain and doing what they both felt was necessary in the aftermath of such tragic circumstances.

Only hours after they buried Adrian, Mary Dunne and her family drove to Donegal, to Ciara's hometown of Gort, to see their grandchildren and the daughter-in-law they loved laid to rest. The O'Briens did not attend Adrian's funeral. They are known to be very private and are highly respected within their community. Throughout the media scrum to get to the bottom of what actually happened that sad day, they chose to keep their thoughts to themselves as they struggled to come to terms with the tragedy that had unfolded.

Jim McDaid TD, a family friend of the O'Briens, spoke out on their behalf, saying that, some months earlier, they had spoken to a garda and a nurse in Wexford to raise their concerns over their daughter's health and safety. However, no official complaint was ever received and, unfortunately for them, no contact was ever made with their beloved child and her two little girls.

They also didn't know of the tragedy that had struck the Dunnes just four weeks earlier when Adrian had lost his younger brother.

James's death had devastated Adrian but, according to his mother, he was more annoyed that his brother had taken his life than anything else.

'James had been away for ten years and would only come home the odd weekend,' says Mary. 'They weren't very close as children, they were just too alike and they clashed. They couldn't get on at all. Even as they grew older, they fought. James couldn't take any criticism and Adrian would call him a fool and they'd row and not talk for ages. And that's the way they always were. But James was very depressed, not like Adrian who was fine as far as I'm concerned. James kept saying to me that he wanted to self-harm and he was very low but he wouldn't get help. I'd say to him go up to the doctor, talk so someone, but on the day he'd be due to go, he'd say he was feeling OK. But he wasn't OK. He couldn't see any way forward for himself at all.

'But Adrian was one of the last people James spoke to before he took his own life on the Saturday. James had gone downhill after he split up with his girlfriend some months before and he couldn't get over it. He had given up his job and he just didn't seem to care about anything anymore. Himself and Adrian had fallen out over something stupid and the night before he died, he rang Adrian to apologise. They were talking for three or four hours on the phone that night. Adrian said that James was rambling on and not making much sense, but that he seemed OK by the time he put the phone down. But James took his own life the next day. His brother Cornelius found him. He had hanged himself out in the shed with a sheet from the clothes line. Myself and Cornelius took him down, tried to bring him back, but we were too late.'

Mary says the whole family was devastated by James's death. 'It's the last thing you want to happen to your child,' she says. She remembers, though, that Adrian was very annoyed with James for what he had done and started shouting at her saying that James had been selfish to kill himself, especially because Mary had been sick. She tried to explain to Adrian that James wasn't well, but Adrian wouldn't listen and was still annoyed that James had committed suicide and left everyone else to pick up the pieces. 'That's what baffles me even more about Adrian's death,' says Mary, 'he was so against doing anything like that.'

Mary knows the media—and people in general—made a lot out of the fact that Adrian and Ciara made quite specific funeral arrangements but thinks there was an overreaction to this. She has done the same thing, as has her daughter, Bridget, and, as Mary says, that doesn't mean Bridget is going to hurt herself. 'It's just something we've talked about over the years, that we were going to make arrangements for our own funerals. I'd said that funerals are getting so dear that I would make my own arrangements. And I went along and I did it.'

Mary still believes that Adrian and Ciara may have been telling the truth when they said that they were only making arrangements, because they did worry about Ciara having a car accident and that they'd all be killed in it. She says a lot was made of the fact that Adrian and Ciara had specified what their daughters should wear if they died before they were six—but, she says, they didn't say the children would die before they were six.

She admits she doesn't know what happened, she wishes she did. 'If I knew, I'd be great but I don't. But I don't blame Ciara and I don't blame Adrian. They were a loving family and they loved one another and they loved their children too much to do any harm to them. Adrian will probably be put down as a murderer but I know that he was no murderer. I do know that if he did do it—he didn't do it on his own. He was totally blind. It would be bad enough to try and do that if you have your sight or if you have a bit of sight. If you were after killing two children and killing your wife, you'd be frustrated enough, even if you had your sight. But for a totally blind person to be able to go back and find a place to hang himself, in my eyes that's not possible. And it's not just that he was my son, regardless of whose son he was I'd still say the same.'

Mary says that her life has been turned upside down since the four bodies were found. She finds it hard to sleep and has been hospitalised because of concerns about her heart and her general health. Mary had had a very tough time before the bodies of her son's family were found. Her husband had died in April 2006, James was buried on 1 April 2007 and then Adrian and his family were found three weeks later on 23 April. As Mary says, 'It's not easy to take that kind of pressure.' She says her faith in God has helped her get through everything. 'I do believe that God helps you. God gives it to you and he takes it away from you too, and we're all given crosses to bear in life, but I don't think I could get over a lot more. The house went on fire three times and we lost everything, but we lost a lot more by losing their lives.'

She remembers how her family was still in shock from James's death and was still grieving for him when Adrian and his family were found.

'I'll never forget that day as long as I live. I was down in the Lochrann Centre in Wexford when I heard. It's a centre for the visually impaired. Bridget had rung her brother Cornelius and he told her to tell me that there was a rumour going around that Adrian, Ciara and the children were all dead. I couldn't believe it and said they must have been codding and it must have been another family that were dead and they just got it wrong.'

But when Mary tried to ring Adrian she couldn't get through. She had tried ringing him earlier that morning to organise something for the children, but hadn't got an answer then either. When she couldn't get him on the phone, the people from the Lochrann Centre brought her back to Monageer and, when she got into the housing estate, it was all blocked off. She could see guards outside Adrian's house. 'No one came to tell us they were dead, we were told nothing. But we knew from the fact that we couldn't get near the house that something bad had happened. We never got to see the bodies of Ciara and the children. I never saw any of them after they died, and we were never given any reason for not seeing them either.'

The only member of the family who did see the bodies was Sebastian, who identified the four bodies when he went to the hospital. 'It was very hard for him to have to do that,' says Mary, 'but he did it.'

'People say that Adrian may have been depressed over James's death,' she continues, 'and that's why he did what they say he did, but I don't think James's death or his daddy's death had anything to do with it. And I don't believe it had anything to do with the girls' sight either. Adrian was well able to cope with the girls' sight, and so was Ciara. Other people have suggested that Ciara might have wanted to leave Adrian but that would never have entered my mind because they were too close for anything like that.'

As a child, Adrian had suffered from epileptic attacks—at times these had left him rigid on the floor and unable to move—and he was on a high dose of prescription drugs to curtail them. However, contrary to media reports at the time, stating that he had recently stopped taking his medication, his mother says that he had stopped taking the drugs years earlier, before he met Ciara, because he was unhappy with the drowsy feelings he experienced when he took them. Mary says his doctor was aware that he had stopped taking his medication and she wasn't aware of him having had any attacks in the months or years after. She refutes any suggestion that her son may have been depressed because he was suffering withdrawal symptoms from his medication.

She also believes that her son loved his children too much to take their lives.

'Adrian and Ciara loved those girls. And Adrian was well able to care for them even though he was blind. He would change their nappies when they were younger, bath them and make their breakfasts. He lived for them children. I never heard him complain about his life.

'Lean was the light of his life. He was so delighted when she was born. They were living in Letterkenny at the time and I went to clean up the place for Ciara coming home with the baby and by the time I got there, he had it all done. It was like a new pin. He was well able to manage things. Adrian always loved kids. He used to look after his two little nieces when they lived here with me. That's why I cannot imagine him hurting two little ones, his own children. In my mind, he wouldn't have it in him to hurt his own children. He'd often ring up and ask me how to cook things, or if one of the children were sick he'd ask me what to do, but other than that I left them to live their own lives, I tried not to interfere. If they needed me, they knew where I was. That's the way I am with all of my children.'

Mary misses her two granddaughters every day, as does everyone else in her family. She talks fondly about them and how playful they were. She also remembers how well the girls got on together, how they loved playing together and playing with their cousins at Mary's house.

Like all children, the two girls loved to play out on the slide and on the swings, but their father was afraid to let them play outside. He was worried that something would happen to them because of their short vision. Mary says that when the family lived in Monageer, some of the other kids would throw stones and he was afraid of the girls getting hit. The two girls had had regular eye operations and Adrian was terrified that something would happen to them. 'You could say he was a bit overprotective for the children's sake,' she says, 'but he was trying to mind them. When he used to come up home here, he could let them go loose. There was no one to harm them.'

Mary describes how they often went to Adrian's house for the family's birthdays and how they would all celebrate with a party. Mary and her husband, Hughie, also had 'bits of parties' in their own house. 'The family would be there and you'd have a few drinks and Hughie, God rest him, would play a bit of music or I'd sing a few songs or some of the rest of the lads would sing a few songs, that kind of a thing.'

Four of the nine children Mary Dunne gave birth to suffered from a hereditary eye disease and had either partial or full blindness. Her husband was totally blind when he died of a heart attack in 2006. However, the children's disability did result in them having a fairly sheltered childhood, and they had very few friends in the area where they grew up. Mary feels society was responsible for the restricted lifestyle that Adrian and his siblings became accustomed to.

'I'm hurt by how the children were treated when they were growing up,' she says. 'The abuse from other children, the name calling. We heard after the lads died that some people in Monageer would call Adrian and the girls "the three blind mice" when they'd come out of the house. That's so hurtful.'

However, Mary has more worries about the future, 'I'm hurt too to know that the children coming on in the world now, my grandchildren, that they're going to be hurt much more than mine were ever hurt, because years down what are they going to hear? "Oh, their uncle killed his wife and children." It's not going to be easy for a young one to put up with that kind of a stigma. And we'll not be known as just the blind Dunnes anymore, they'll be adding in that we have a murderer in the family as well.

'It's very hard, but it's the truth, and I said it here at the time of the funeral and at the time of the wake. I said I pity the children. I pity myself all right, for what I have to go through now, but it's nothing to what those poor children are going to have to go through in years to come. They don't mind how hard they hurt you or how hard they hit you. I've been there, I know what it's like.'

When locals started whispering about what could have made Adrian carry out such horrific murders, killing his whole family, his illness and that of his two little girls was the first thing to be considered for the carefully planned execution.

But Mary Dunne disagrees with the suggestion.

'He coped with everything throughout his life up to that and I don't see how he could have suddenly decided he'd had enough. He was stronger than that. People will talk anyway and say what they like, trying to come up with reasons why they think Adrian would do something like that, but I saw him fight off his epilepsy, he took it in his stride, and he took anything that came his way in his stride. Even when he lost his eye when he was just seven, he took that in his stride. Losing the second eye hit him a little bit because he had no sight at all then and he had to be dependent on people to bring him everywhere. But he got through it. And he was going to be there for his little girls if they lost their sight.'

―――

Adrian didn't have a guide dog because Ciara didn't like dogs. Instead he used a cane but as she brought him everywhere, he didn't use that much—and when Ciara started to drive, they went everywhere in the car.

'She wouldn't let him out of her sight,' says Mary. 'And that's why I cannot see either of them harming each other, they loved each other. People might say I'm saying that because I'm his mother but if I was looking at this as someone other than Adrian Dunne's mother, and I knew the man the way I knew Adrian, I would still say he couldn't have done it.'

Mary and her family are annoyed at the way her family found out about the deaths of Adrian and his family. At the lack of respect shown. 'We were never approached by the gardaí or anyone else to tell us what had happened. The lads only heard it as a rumour around the pub and then some of them heard it on the radio. That was how we heard and how we went up to the house that day. No one officially told us.'

Adrian's brother, Cornelius agrees. 'It was very hard for me to break the news to my mother that they were all dead,' he says, 'and I'm very bitter over the fact that I had to do it and not the guards. It took a friend of mine to tell me and I had to tell my ma. It was very difficult because it was so soon after James's death. As the saying goes, a paper never refused ink. Some people will believe whatever they read in the papers but sometimes they are wrong. On the morning of the tragedy, I was in Wexford and the first thing we were told was that they had found a gun in the house, now when I first heard that it made me laugh, a blind man with a gun. But that's how stupid people are. They'll believe anything.'

The weekend that the Adrian and his family died, Mary was in Cork with her daughter, Bridget. She was still upset about James's death and so Bridget had suggested they go away together to get a break from what was happening. However, Mary's sons were still in Wexford and nobody contacted them to suggest that they were worried about the way Adrian and Ciara had been behaving. 'When I went away that weekend,' Mary says, 'to get over the death of one son, I didn't think that I'd be coming back to find another four of my family dead.

'My life changed the day Hugh died, and then again when I lost James, but nothing could be worse for me than losing Adrian and the children. I'd give anything to have them back with me. But, unfortunately, I can't change what's happened. I lost a baby, Vernon, when he was only seven weeks old, he had a cot death, and it's heartbreaking to lose a child at any age, but I'm totally heartbroken over those two little girls.

'To be honest I'm a bit wary of everybody. I don't really trust anybody. It's hard to trust people unless you really know them. Your best friend could be your worst enemy. I don't bother with going anywhere now myself, not since Hugh died. I have friends all right, people ring me and we talk on the phone, but in regards to going out places, I don't go. Adrian and Ciara were probably much the same, they didn't bother going out anywhere and they felt happy enough at home. We kept it among ourselves and maybe we were our own worst enemies that we didn't go out and mix with other people, or get other people to mix with us, but sure you can't make anyone do anything. That's the way I look at it.'

———

Adrian's brother, Cornelius, is now in counselling following the death of two brothers, a sister-in-law and two little nieces in the space of a month. He believes, like his mother, that Adrian was in no way responsible for the deaths of his family and he feels the reports conducted into their deaths can never prove beyond doubt who killed the family.

'I was the last person to see James alive,' he says. 'And I hadn't even started to get over his death when we lost Adrian and the family. Both my brothers were older than me and it's hard to lose two of your big brothers, and in such a short time. But although they may not be here physically, they're always going to be here spiritually in my life. I know they're up there looking down on me, them and my da and all my family members that have gone. Adrian was a great father, even though he was totally blind. He raised them girls when people doubted he could do it. He proved everyone wrong. Unfortunately, they were cut down in their prime. The girls were so bright, he had them doing Irish and saying their prayers every night.'

Cornelius remembers that when his dad was alive Adrian would ring at about 9 p.m. and Lean would come to the phone and say,

"Grandad, say my prayers with me", and they would say their prayers and count from one to ten in Irish before she went to sleep. This is something that happened every night. His nieces always had smiles on their faces and would cheer people up just by looking at them.

However, Cornelius felt sorry for the family living in Monageer. He says Adrian and Ciara didn't want to let their daughters play out the front of their house because people would throw stones at them. 'It was very hard for them,' he says. 'I'm not going to judge people in Monageer, but I know how they felt living there.'

Cornelius often called down to the family when they lived in New Ross—before the moved to Monageer. He says Ciara was a great cook and used to cook food for an army. Whenever he called down to them, he always got a good feed.

Like Mary, Cornelius only has his memories left of the good times the family had together. 'I recorded Lean's last birthday party before she died and that's my little memory of everyone. I have her playing on the bouncy castle and just being a happy child. They're my memories of the two small girls. They loved Dora and Barney and even though they were only young they were big Liverpool supporters and they loved the Wexford hurling team. I remember on Lean's birthday, I rang Adrian's phone and pretended that I was Barney but she knew immediately and she said, "You're not Barney, you're Uncle Diddley." You know that's a good memory and I just wish I had more and that they hadn't died the way they did, so young.'

Cornelius also doesn't think the truth about what happened will ever be known. 'In my mind either the two of them, Adrian and Ciara, did it or there was a third party. But I don't know who that third party could have been. It just seems more likely that it was someone else because Adrian and Ciara loved the kids so much and I just can't see them harming them.'

But the inquiry firmly ruled out a third party involvement in the deaths. 'They said Adrian did it and although I can't believe he could do something like that, I'll just have to accept it.'

Cornelius also hopes that now his mother will be allowed some peace and allowed to mourn. 'I personally haven't even got over my dad's death yet. God only knows what's going to happen for us all in the future but all I can hope for is that we get some sort of closure on all of this.'

Mary knows life will never be the same again.

'There's not a day that goes by when I don't think of them all,' she says. 'But no matter what, I could never think of Adrian as killing his wife and his children and himself, because that would not be the person that I knew. But when the inquest comes out I'll just have to accept whatever it says. But the only thing in that inquest that will mean anything to me will be the fact that they can give us an exact time of death so that at least we'll be able to put a date on the headstone for him. Maybe then we can try to get our lives someway back together. But our family will never be the same again, because there's so many of us missing now. And I wouldn't wish this on anyone.'

The Monageer Report stated that while there were many services of the Health Board and other agencies working with the family, the inquiry team did not identify any one key worker who had access to all of the information. It recommended that the provision of a national out-of-hours service be structured and resourced to ensure an appropriate response to all serious child protection and welfare concerns.

——

Nearly a year to the day after the Dunne tragedy another family in Clonroche were found dead in their beautiful home.

Initially, it was thought that successful, handsome businessman, Diarmuid Flood, his beautiful blonde wife and former beauty queen, Lorraine, and their two children, Mark and Julie, had all died in a tragic house fire. But further examination showed no signs of a break-in and forensic examinations proved that both parents had been shot and that Lorraine's wound was not self-inflicted. It was also discovered that both children had been killed in their beds before the fire. It is thought that Diarmuid decided to kill himself and to take his family with him, the horror of which is something that both families will have to live with.

While many suicidal parents, who go on to kill their children, show signs of distress in advance, this is frequently not enough to alert even close relatives. To other family members, Ciara and Adrian were happy with their life together. Apart from money worries, just like most other young couples today, they continued as normal with family life. Earlier that week, they had driven to Courtown, a seaside resort not too far away, for a family outing. Nothing appeared to be out of character.

There have been a number of killings that could possibly have been prevented if intervention had taken place at the right time.

- In January 2007, Eileen Murphy threw herself from the Cliffs of Moher, taking her four-year-old son, Evan, to his death with her. The distraught mum left behind a note to say she was sorry. She had made her plans carefully, travelling from her home in County Cork to Galway the night before and then taking a tour bus to the cliffs. Incredibly, little Evan survived the fall but died later from the injuries he sustained.
- In February 2006, Mary Keegan stabbed to death her two sons, Glenn (ten) and Andrew (six), before turning the knife on herself at their home at Firhouse in Dublin. At the inquests into the deaths, Brian Keegan, Mary's grieving husband, said his wife had become engulfed in a serious depression, although he had not realised it. He described her at the time as a loving and generous person and an inspiration to himself and his two boys. He said he bore no anger in his heart towards her.
- In April 2005, a mother of three, Sharon Grace, drowned herself and her two young daughters Mikaela (four) and Abby (three) off Kaats Strand in County Wexford. A short time earlier, the troubled woman had tried to speak to a social worker at a Wexford hospital but was told there was no one available. Sharon had been estranged from her husband, Barry, for months previously.
- In November 2001, Canadian George McGloin (32), a medical technician working in Limerick, stabbed his two-year-old

daughter in the neck just hours after he was seen laughing and playing with her in Callan, County Kilkenny. He then killed himself with the same kitchen knife. He had been separated from his wife, Lorraine Leahy, and the two children and had had a row with her over an access visit. When he hit Lorraine on the back of the head with a poker, she ran out of the house for help but he was then able to block neighbours from entering the house before he killed his child and then himself.

- In August 2001, six-year-old Deirdre Crowley was shot dead by her father, Christopher, after he had snatched her from her mother, Christine O'Sullivan. He had managed to keep his daughter hidden for two years and when gardaí finally discovered his hiding place, he killed his daughter and then turned the gun on himself. He had carefully drawn up the abduction plan, selling his house and clearing out his bank accounts. For two years, Christine had made repeated appeals for help in finding Deirdre and was even told she was about to be reunited with her hours before Crowley killed her daughter.

- In July 2001, Greg Fox murdered his wife, Debbie, and sons, Trevor (nine) and Killian (seven). The couple's marriage had been in trouble and Debbie had reportedly confided to friends that splitting up with her jealous husband 'wouldn't be easy'. Fox had moved out of the family home for a few weeks but had returned home determined to try and keep his family together. When he realised that this was not possible, he viciously attacked Debbie and then repeatedly stabbed his children.

In recent years, family tragedies on the scale of that of Adrian and Ciara Dunne have been occurring with appalling regularity in Ireland.

08 | A SLOW DEATH

BRIAN STACK

When Sheila and Brian Stack married in September 1967, life could not have been better for them. They had first met at a dance in their hometown of Portlaoise a couple of years earlier and the relationship had developed from there. Brian was already working as a prison officer in the town and Sheila was a secretary for Bradshaws, a local motor parts company.

Brian first's job in the prison service was in Dublin's Mountjoy Prison in 1959. He loved his work and was determined to get to the top as quickly as possible. Just three years after they married, he was promoted and transferred to Cork Prison. By then the couple had three little boys, Austin, Kieran and Oliver, and so the whole family packed up and headed south.

Three years later, Brian was moved once again, this time to Limerick, but a short time later, he was promoted and the family returned to Portlaoise, happy that they were back for good. Their home was on the outskirts of the town and they had a large network of friends from both the prison service and the local community.

Brian rose through the ranks of the prison swiftly and, by 1983, was the most senior uniformed officer there. His job meant everything to him.

Throughout the 1970s and 1980s, Portlaoise Prison was home to many prominent IRA members and was a tense environment to control at the best of times. There had been a number of attempted breakouts and, in 1974, to the embarrassment of the prison service, 19 prisoners succeeded in escaping. With tensions rising, and to avoid further embarrassment, security was at an all-time high.

Officers had to be extra vigilant and, in 1975, their efforts paid off when they foiled a break out by firing a number of shots over the prisoners' heads, as they attempted to free themselves by using explosives that had been smuggled into the prison days before. The problem of smuggling had become so bad that a policy of strip-searching prisoners was implemented.

However, despite the pressure he was under as a leading officer in command, Brian Stack never allowed his work to interfere with his family life and spent all the time he could with his three boys, playing football, hurling or boxing. His motto was 'what happens in work, stays in work' and he never bothered his wife with his worries.

———

Brian was sports mad and, at 47 years of age, had just received his international boxing refereeing licence. On the night of Friday, 25 March 1983, he attended the Irish Senior Boxing Championships at the National Stadium on the South Circular Road in Dublin. It was outside of this venue that his life changed in the most dramatic of ways.

As he left the stadium to meet up with his friends for the trip home, he started chatting and was congratulating one of the boxers on his fight that night. Brian had spent the evening walking around the arena, catching up with trainers and young boxers from all over the country. When he had said his last goodbyes to those at the stadium at roughly 10.50 p.m., he crossed the South Circular Road and headed towards Washington Street, where some of his friends were waiting in the car.

They were heading, as usual, to Joels' Restaurant on the Naas Road, something they did after ever fight they attended at the stadium. However, as Brian walked down Washington Street, he became aware that he was being followed by someone wearing a balaclava. As he got near his friends' car, the masked assailant quickened his pace to catch up. When he was right behind Brian, he casually raised the .38 inch revolver and, at point-blank range, fired a shot straight into the base of Brian Stack's head.

After the single shot was fired, Brian slumped to the ground, his suit and overcoat immediately drenched in blood. His friends, including the young son of one of Brian's friends, looked on in disbelief and shock at what they had just seen. Within seconds of the hit, a motorbike appeared at the corner of the road and the gunman made his getaway. As the high-powered bike took off at speed in the direction of Leonard's Corner, it narrowly missed an oncoming car. The following day a black, grey and red Kawasaki z400J, was dragged from the Grand Canal at Portobello, it had been stolen from Pimlico in Dublin two months earlier in January. Officers believe this vehicle was the bike the assassins used to escape from the scene.

On the night of the attack, Brian's friends stood on the side of the road in horror and watched him struggle to survive. Doctors from Northern Ireland attending the fight raced across the road on hearing what had happened and battled to save Brian's life by giving him mouth-to-mouth resuscitation and putting pressure on the blood flow from the gunshot wound in his head. They kept him alive until the ambulance arrived.

The shot did not kill Brian that night. Instead, it left him in agony for 18 long months. It stole his personality, his family and it left him totally dependent on those around him. The bullet had severely damaged his spinal cord leaving him a quadriplegic with no control over his bladder or bowel. When the doctors were battling to save his life on Washington Street, his heart had stopped and, though he was eventually resuscitated, the loss of oxygen to the brain for those immediate moments is believed to have caused the severity of brain damage that left him totally incapacitated.

His injuries meant that Sheila and their boys now had to look after a husband and a dad who now had the intellect of a five-year-old.

As Brian Stack battled for his life that night at the Meath Hospital, gardaí from Kevin Street Garda Station were trying to piece together what had happened, seeking motives for the hit. The most likely motive, as far as gardaí were concerned, was that the attack was ordered by a former prisoner looking for revenge for something that may have happened in the prison under Brian's watch—either that or it was a direct warning from Republicans to stop meddling in their affairs by increasing security checks in the prison, thereby hampering the smuggling of contraband goods.

However, Sheila Stack had a different view. Initially, she toyed with the idea that the shooting could have had something to do with an argument over a decision at a boxing match, because it happened outside the stadium, but she quickly discounted this. Then her mind turned to the issue that had been tormenting her husband for months before, a work-related issue that had nothing to do with troublesome prisoners. Sheila knew that he had been worrying incessantly about something but she never for one moment thought that whatever was bothering him could ultimately lead to his death.

'Brian had been very, very tense in the months leading up to the shooting,' she says. 'I'd ask him what was wrong with him but he would just say, "I'm working on something and don't ask me any more questions."'

'I felt myself that whatever was going on, it was way outside the remit of his everyday work practice. But at the same time, he was not prepared to go much further. I didn't worry too much over it because I didn't think that he was personally in danger. I just thought it was a work thing and it would blow over. But at the time of the shooting, he was a completely different man to how he was maybe six months prior to that. He never normally brought problems home from work or spoke about them, but I started querying him asking him what was wrong, saying, "You're not talking, you know? Is it something I've done?" And he just said,

"It's nothing got to do with anybody, it's work related. I'm having a lot of hassle at work. I'm working on something and I want to get to the bottom of it. It's nothing got to do with you and I don't want to talk about it any further for now."'

Sheila knows he was tense and acting out of character. Her husband was a man who was quiet and caring and didn't speak very much anyway. He always saw himself as the provider in the home, and believed that he was there to make sure that everything was provided for and that his family were never short of anything. Domestically, he did nothing, that was Sheila's job, but he did take care of his sons and always wanted them to be involved.

'Sport was a big factor in our lives,' says Sheila, 'and if anything sporty was going on, we'd be there. And that was a sense of relaxation for us all, how we'd all wind down. After that, Brian would go for 40 winks or watch a small bit of television.'

She remembers that her husband would occasionally speak about the dangers of his job and would always say that he had to have eyes in the back of his head and had to be conscious of his surroundings as best as he could, but be as relaxed as he could too, without making it too obvious. 'I don't know if he was ever threatened,' she says, 'he may have been and just never said, but he always told me to be careful of who was around me just in case they recognised him. But he always respected former prisoners. A few times when we were on holiday, we'd have had people coming up to him asking him for a few bob for a pint and he would say, "Oh that was so and so, he was in the custody of the state at some stage." But he never put them down to me.'

This is one reason Sheila doesn't think Brian was shot by a former prisoner. He had so much on his mind in relation to something at work at the time, that in Sheila's mind—in all her family's mind—the motive for trying to take Brian's life had something to do with work, and not the prisoners.

———

Sheila was in bed when the knock came to the door to say her husband had been shot. The family had planned a day out to Newry the following morning and she had gone to bed earlier than usual so she would be ready for the early start. When she opened the door, she was surprised to find her brother standing in front of her with a worried look on his face.

'He just came in and said that Brian was in an accident in Dublin,' she recalls. 'It could have been about 11 p.m. He said that one of the guards had come down to him and told him. He said, "I don't know any more than that but I'll go off and find out and see what I can get and come back to you." So I was left there wondering what had happened—was Brian badly hurt? I don't know how long it was before my brother came back with my mother and another brother of mine who was living in town, he then told me the full story. My first reaction was shock. I thought it must have been some fellow arguing over a decision that had been made at a fight or something like that.'

The guards arrived at the house shortly after but didn't give the family much information, so Sheila and her brothers went to Dublin and, by 2 a.m., they had arrived at the Meath Hospital. 'I was very calm at the time,' says Sheila, 'I think I must have been in shock. Brian was in ICU and they explained to me that they would have to take him to theatre to remove the bullet. We saw him before he went down and the only thing we noticed was that his whole body was very swollen, especially his head, it was about double its normal size. The doctors didn't think he would pull through that night. And that was very hard to take. The outlook was very bleak as the hours went by. But then they informed us that it wasn't as bad as they had initially thought and he might just be paralysed in one arm. But, as time went on, things manifested differently.'

As Sheila waited for her husband to come out of surgery, all she could think about was why someone had wanted to kill him. She then began to think through different scenarios. Was he going to be OK? If he did pull through, could he go back to work? Was he just going to be paralysed in one arm? She felt that that wouldn't have been too difficult to cope with. But her main worry was about getting him well again, but the doctors couldn't give her any guarantees. She felt the whole situation was one of doom and gloom.

When he came out of surgery, Brian was in a coma for about three months. Every day Sheila thought and hoped that he might wake up, however, when he eventually did, he was a very different person. 'I was in the National Rehabilitation Hospital in Dún Laoghaire on the evening that he woke up and his eyes were just all over the place. He didn't seem to recognise me at all but my sister, Catherine, was with me and he recognised her. He got a few words out after a long period of time, and he asked her who I was. It put a lump in my throat to be honest with you, it was very difficult to take.

'In days after that, he remembered nothing really. He just wanted to know where he was and he wasn't aware of his condition or anything. It took a while for him to realise something was wrong and he seemed to think that he was at a football game and that he was pushed into the goals.

'Nobody prepared us for what we had to deal with. Brian had the intellectual ability of a five-year-old child. We never realised how bad his brain damage would be. And we just took it day by day; that was the way the dice fell. It took him a while to recognise the boys as well and on the day he finally did, there were a lot of tears. It was bedlam. The boys were only 14, 13 and 12 at the time. Oliver ran out of the room, he was so upset, but we had the doctors there for support that day and that helped, but it was a horrific experience for us all. Brian cried as well because he saw how his children reacted to the change in him. It was an odd situation because he had lost his short-term memory but he still remembered some things from in the past.'

Sheila had to put all of her emotions to the back of her head and concentrate on nursing her husband back to health. She had to forget about Brian being her partner and treat him as if he was a patient. It was essential that she kept on top of things at home for the sake of her children because, at that time, she didn't know how things would turn out as the days and weeks passed. 'It was very, very difficult because you couldn't converse as you would normally,' she says.

The staff at the Rehabilitation Hospital suggested to Sheila that Brian should go home, they thought it might be good for his stimulation, but it didn't make much difference. Sheila says Brian knew he was home, he was aware of his surroundings and was glad to be home. However, his personality didn't revert to that of the man she had lived with before the shooting. Brian became an aggressive and angry person, and was very demanding. 'When he wanted something done, he wanted it done right now,' remembers Sheila, 'regardless of the circumstances, and the whole house had to revolve around him. It was hell!'

Sheila says that Brian didn't speak about the shooting. There were times when he could talk to her normally—not quite the way he had before the shooting, but he could talk. But he didn't remember what had happened when he was shot and never talked about what he was investigating in the prison.

Brian and Sheila never discussed their new situation with his illness. But then, one day out of the blue, Brian said, '"Look what I have done to the family because of my work.' Sheila says it was like he would 'come and go'. But she never blamed him for what had happened, she doesn't think he had any control over events. 'As far as we are all concerned, he was a good man and was doing his job the best he could and someone wanted him to stop. We all had to pay the price. Brian had so many things wrong with him when he came home. His breathing was a big issue. He had to go on a manual ventilator every day, twice a day, because his chest was so badly damaged. A lot of nights I sat there and thought that it would have been better if he were not to survive that night, for everybody's sake because it was very, very difficult.'

The specialists didn't give Sheila any idea of how long her husband might live, but she knew in her own heart that she was losing him bit by bit and that it was only really a matter of time before he died of the complications brought on by his injuries.

'His breathing was just getting worse and worse,' she recalls.

'One night when things were really bad', I called the doctor. I was on my own and I was very scared. The doctor gave him an injection, he said it would make him relax and he might get some sleep, because he had been up all night. But when the doctor left that night, his breathing seemed to get slower and slower. I got very angry, very annoyed and very nervous because I was just there on my own and trying to cope with everything. I ran up to a neighbour who was a nurse and she came down. Between the two of us, we got him out of the chair and put him down on the floor and she did mouth to mouth resuscitation on him and called the ambulance.'

That night, Brian was taken to the local hospital and, after a few days, he was moved back to the Meath Hospital in Dublin. He had fallen back into a coma and the doctors told Sheila that he would never come out of it. The staff wouldn't let Sheila take Brian home, even with a 24-hour nurse, so the Rehabilitation Hospital in Dún Laoghaire agreed to care for him again. However, as plans were being made to transfer him, Brian died.

It was Saturday, 29 September 1984, 18 months after Brian had been brutally gunned down on a Dublin street.

Sheila and the children were devastated that the man they all loved so much was finally gone from them forever. In some way, though, they were also slightly relieved that he would no longer have to exist in such a painful and heartbreaking way.

Brian had a huge state funeral in his hometown, attended by then Taoiseach Garret FitzGerald and then Minister for Justice Michael Noonan. His coffin was draped with the Tricolour. His fellow colleagues north and south of the border were there to honour him and two of his children, Oliver and Kieran, said readings at the mass. For Sheila, it was the end of a long and arduous battle. The man she had loved all those years, for better or for worse in sickness and in health, was finally laid to rest, but the man who took his life was still walking the streets. That broke her heart.

To this day, Brian Stack is the only prison officer in the history of the state to have been murdered. At the time of his murder, the death sentence was still in place for the killing of a garda, a member of the judiciary or a prison officer. Yet despite a huge investigation no one has ever been charged.

'After he was shot, we always knew that Brian was going to die,' says Sheila. 'We just had to make the best of the circumstances. At the time, the boys were away in school as boarders five days a week. Their lives were being messed about no end. I think Brian liked to see them come home at weekends, though, and they'd talk to him and tell them what they had been doing all week. But it had been very hard for them to see their father like that, especially because he had been so active before the shooting. And to this day, it hurts myself and the children to know that no one has ever been charged with his murder. It's hard when we know that it was most likely someone he knew and worked with who organised it, because that is what we believe.'

———

'In the months before his murder, Brian Stack had confided in a friend that he was investigating something within the prison and that, if it was true, it would rock the foundation of the state,' says Mick Mc Caffrey, news editor with the *Sunday Tribune*. 'There was a rumour in the prison at the time that a staff member within the prison service was on the payroll of the IRA and that that person had become aware that Brian Stack was on to what was happening. This particular person couldn't take the risk that they could be exposed, so they decided to have him murdered.'

There were also allegations that Brian was aware of a plot that Republican prisoners were hatching to organise an escape from the prison. And two years after he died, in November 1985, prison officers once again foiled an escape attempt. The prisoners who organised the breakout were well organised and had prison keys, guns, ammunition and a large amount of Semtex. Rumours surfaced once again that someone 'inside' was aiding the escape attempt. But only Brian Stack can tell if this was the plot he was trying to uncover—the plot that cost him his life.

'At one stage when Brian was in the Meath Hospital, the guards called me over to the station and asked me to make a statement,' says Sheila. 'I told them that I would not discount Brian's colleagues as having been involved with his shooting and they kind of all perked up on their chairs and said, "Why would you make a statement like that?" I told them that he was having a lot of issues at work and I said, "It could be staff related." But I certainly didn't think at that time that it might have been subversives or anybody else, I was more focused on staff issues at that time, that it was someone in work who didn't like it that Brian was getting too close to what they were up to and they had to sort him out.'

——

Despite what happened to his father, Brian's eldest son, Austin, followed his dad into the prison service. It was a worry to his mother because she was aware of how some people had reacted when she claimed that it may have been someone within the service who ordered the hit on her husband. But Austin was proud of his dad and the work he did and was eager to follow in his footsteps.

When he joined the service, his father's colleagues, and prisoners, inundated Austin with stories about his father and about the type of person he was.

'I was working recently in Limerick Prison and I met an awful lot of officers down there who worked with my father,' says Austin. 'He worked there in the late 1970s and he was there again for a short period in 1980s and of all the people I've spoken to, I've never come across anybody who had a bad word to say about him, and that includes prisoners and ex-prisoners.'

Austin heard how his father had organised a football team in Limerick Prison soon after he arrived. Sheila then found a photograph of the 1977 prison football team, with the governor of Limerick at the time in it. Austin brought the picture in to the governor who told him a story about how his father had organised the match with a Limerick firm and that he refereed it himself because he was an inter-county referee at the time. At one point, the prison service was losing the match and Brian kept playing for time until the officers got a draw and then he blew for full-time. Brian then got sponsorship for the team so that they'd have proper kits and jerseys. 'He was also involved in training younger staff,' says Austin, 'and I've met a number of them who would have encountered him maybe on their first or second day in the job and they all would say to me how nice he was to them and how comfortable they made them feel.

'It was the same with any prisoners I have spoken to who knew him. In fact, one prisoner told me how my father would get him out every year for the Horse Show in Dublin, on day release. This guy wasn't a paramilitary prisoner, just an ordinary working prisoner, but he told me how good my father was to them and how he respected everyone. So I don't put much weight on the theory that somebody had a grudge against him.

'I was only young when my father died but I remember a couple of things he said to me about the prisoners. He'd say that while their liberty has been taken away from them, you've always got to remember that you're dealing with human beings. He also said, "Never, ever promise something to a prisoner that you can't deliver on, if you're going to make a promise to a guy who's incarcerated, you've got to be able to follow that through." I suppose it's something that I've taken on board as a prison officer myself in a management position, that you should never actually promise something to a guy that you can't deliver.'

Austin says that knowing the type of man his father was, he doesn't think what happened to him had anything to do with a grudge. He also thinks that his father was shot because of an issue related to his job—that someone wanted him out of the way in case something came out that could damage their reputation.

'I miss my father a lot. I have great memories of him from my childhood. He was an extremely affectionate man. If I was in trouble in school, for example, and my mother had told him that night what had happened, the next morning, he'd climb into the bed beside me and put his arm around me and ask what had happened. No shouting or roaring, he'd just ask. And when he'd come in from work in the evenings, he'd sit down for a few minutes for a nap and when he'd wake he'd jump up, tog off into his football shorts and a football jersey and go out the back and get into the whole spirit of paying a game of football with you.

'If we wanted something and my mother had said no to us, to wait until our birthday or Christmas, he'd put a few bob by every week and he'd get it for us. I remember he did it once with a tent for Oliver and me, and we were thrilled. He was always thinking of us and looking out for us. When he came home from the prison, he was a different Brian Stack to what I imagine he would have been like in work. He was a real family man and he never really talked about work.

'I was only 14 when it all happened, but I remember it all very well. The night before the shooting, Kieran, Oliver and myself were badgering my father to let us go to the stadium with him, but because he was in a car pool with a couple of friends of his, there wouldn't have been room for us to travel up. We were all boxing ourselves at the time and we were very keen to go, but we were going on a shopping trip up North the following day and he said, "Look we're all heading off tomorrow, so ye go to bed early and we'll all be up early to go to Newry in the morning." So we just agreed with him and he headed off.'

Later that night, Austin, whose bedroom was at the front of the house, was woken by headlights coming in through the window. He heard some people talking in the kitchen and so went downstairs to see what was happening. He saw one of his uncles on the phone and then saw another uncle and his grandmother. They all told him to go back to bed, saying that his father had been hit by a motorbike and they were trying to find out more details. Austin says he was reassured that everything would be OK and that everyone would still be heading up to Newry the following day. He went back to bed but had a restless night because of a nagging feeling that something wasn't right. He felt there were too many people in the house for it not to be serious.

'I used to leave the radio on all night in my bedroom at that stage,' he says. 'I'd go to bed listening to Radio Luxembourg or some of the pirate stations in Dublin. At about 6.30 a.m. the following day, I turned up the radio to hear the news. I switched over to RTÉ 1—which a fellow of 14 at the time wouldn't have done—and it was the first item on the news. It basically said that my father had been shot the night before and that he was in a critical condition in the Meath Hospital. I went down to Kieran and Oliver, who were sharing a bedroom, and I woke them up and I told them what I had heard on the radio but they didn't believe me.

'I switched on the radio and the 7 a.m. news came on and they heard it for themselves. My grandmother had stayed in the house that night because my mother and her two brothers had gone up to Dublin and she had heard us talking in the room, so she came in and she said she had been hoping that we wouldn't hear it on the radio but what we had heard had happened. And that's the way we found out that our father had been shot. We were all in shock that morning. I remember that my grandmother packed us all off into a car and brought us down to mass. And I recall people looking at us a bit funny. And I felt a bit uncomfortable at mass that day with everyone staring at us.'

Austin remembers that, as they sat in church that morning, they didn't know if their father would survive or not. All they knew was that he was critical and things were touch and go. They didn't know the full extent of their father's injuries and only learned some time later that he would be brain damaged and that he was going to be paralysed. When their father was in the coma, they knew that he had kidney failure and had been told that the people in the Meath Hospital were experts in dealing with kidney problems. They were also told that their father had a good chance of surviving because he didn't smoke and rarely drank. 'The fact that he was so fit was another bonus for him. Another man wouldn't have lasted through that night, let alone for 18 months. He was definitely a fighter,' says Austin. 'My mother was very strong through it all as well. She got very little sleep when my father came home. He could wake up in the middle of the night at a whim at maybe 2 a.m. or 3 a.m., and he'd be looking for a glass of water or a glass of milk, or looking for someone to change the position of his head on the pillow, or to move him in the bed and my mother would have to get up in the middle of the night and do that.'

It was a very tough time for Sheila. Although her children did what they could, she was the one looking after Brian the most. She bought a specially adapted car so that they could go out for drives. Sheila wanted to try and bring Brian back, to make him feel better and that he was going somewhere, being a little bit more active. 'We brought him to the county football and hurling finals in Portlaoise, just before he died,' says Austin. 'Portlaoise won the senior county title in football that day and then the following week the hurling finals were on and the GAA let us park the car near the sideline so he could watch the matches. The Portlaoise minors won the hurling that day and all the lads came running over to him in the car with the cup. The senior match was a draw and the replay was a couple of weeks later but by that stage he had passed away.'

The children were in boarding school—the Salesian College Boarding School in Ballinakill—on the day their father fell ill.

'I remember so well the day the headmaster came and told me that something was after happening to my father at home,' says Austin. 'He had been informed by my mother the night before and she asked him to let us have our sleep and break the news to us the following morning. One of the family came over to pick us up from school and brought us back home to Portlaoise. That was on the Thursday and he died on Saturday. He didn't have much time left when he went into the coma for the second time, he died just a couple of days later.

'When I look back now on those 18 months when he was sick, I realise how different things were for us as kids. We were shielded from a lot of what was going on but we were still caught up in it. All of our weekends from school were spent in the hospital at the start and helping out at home when he came home. I remember how, back then, we were all very conscious of being the children of Brian Stack who had been shot and were always very conscious about how people were looking at us. It made us very uncomfortable at times. But speaking for myself, I tried to block all that out and just concentrated on going to school, playing football and getting up to the kind of devilment that all the other young fellows got up to.

'But everything revolved around what my father wanted to do and he could change his mind at the drop of a hat. So it was quite a difficult time. People would come up to us all the time and ask us how our father was and how was he getting on and I'd always say that he was still the same, there was no change, and to this day I don't know if people thought I was putting them off and just not telling them the truth, but that was the reality of it at the time. His condition never changed. It was a very hard time, but we have so many things to be thankful for as well. We had a great father who would do anything for us. He was a great worker and did so much for young people in the area through sport. He died because he was doing his job to the best of his ability and someone wasn't happy. And although I miss him every single day, I am proud to have had him as my father. And I will do everything I can to get to the bottom of what happened to him, who killed him and who ordered it. It's the least I can do as his son.'

Austin's younger brother Kieran also misses his dad being a part of his life as he grows older. He cannot understand how no one has ever been charged with the murder and he just lives with the hope that one day that may change.

'We often chat as a family about how the attack and assassination of our dad has affected us over the past 25 years,' he says. 'I often think, Would our lives have been any different today if our dad was still here? I remember when I was a teenager getting very angry at times about what happened. I remember being in shock for a while and then, of course, you go through denial, thinking, No, this couldn't have happened to us. And then you start asking, "Why us? Why our dad?" But you know over time that mellows a bit but I still get annoyed when I think of all the milestones in our lives that my dad has missed. He wasn't there when we left school, went to college, got married and he never got to see any of his grandchildren. And that hurts.' He is also annoyed that no one has been charged with his father's murder and that his family is still looking for justice.

'Never in our worst nightmares did we think that anything like an assassination could happen to our family. We were only teenagers going through the normal issues teenagers go through, trying to make sense of life, and then this happens. In the midst of everything we have this absolutely traumatic event where out of nowhere our father was taken from us and a husband taken from our mam, not by chance, not by accident but in a very cold, brutal and calculated way by a group of individuals who were clearly motivated.'

Kieran has often wondered if prison officers in the 1970s and 1980s were advised about safety issues. He knows there was a concern over their safety inside and outside of the prison and would like to know what precautions were in place for them. He knows his father never talked to us about it, but he also knows that he must have had his worries. 'At the same time, I would think that because it was such a tense and difficult working environment, that my dad and most of his colleagues used their own common sense, because they would have had to be very cognisant of their own personal safety and of that of their families.'

Kieran remembers that, around the time his dad was shot, members of the prison service in Northern Ireland had been attacked and their families had been targeted. The paramilitaries had suggested that they had a list of names and addresses of prison officers in the Republic and Kieran is sure that people were scared of what may have happened to them or their families. However, he hopes that the Department of Justice and the prison service would have had plans in place to make sure that their members were safe.

'My father never discussed it but I remember how he would be very cautious when we were in Dublin, say going to Croke Park for a game, and he'd be looking around him checking to see if he recognised anyone, former prisoners. I remember at one match, he noticed a few people out of the corner of his eye and in a very discreet and subtle way he said to us, "Kieran, Austin, we'll walk down this street instead." But he never checked under his car for devices or anything like that. I'd say he tried to be as normal as possible for our sakes. But we had seen how bad things could get in the prison for ourselves. As a child, you'd know something was wrong when you heard the prison siren go off and anyone who was off duty would have to go straight back to work. That would happen if there was a riot or something like that.

'One night, we were all in the swimming pool and there was a group of prison officers there and the door was literally taken off the hinges by another officer who rushed in to say that there was a riot in the prison. Everyone jumped out of the pool and put on their clothes without drying themselves. My father put me in the car and drove us up to the prison gates and he parked outside and said, "Look just stay there, I have to go in and see what's going on." About an hour passed and I was still sitting in the front seat of the car when this other officer came out, a young guy, and he had the keys of the car in his hands and he said, "Look your father is after asking me to drive you home, all hell is after breaking loose inside there and it's mad." The siren was going non-stop and there were helicopters flying overhead. But it wasn't anything unusual for us because we knew that was just how it was in my dad's job. We didn't worry about it because it was the norm, we had grown up with it.'

In Portlaoise at the time, there were IRA prisoners, INLA prisoners and a certain number from Saor Éire. It also housed some of the Dublin gangs that were only starting up at the time, such as that of Martin 'The General' Cahill, and then there was a group known as 'ordinary prisoners' who would have been there to do specific cleaning duties. There was no in-cell sanitation at the time as the Provisional IRA refused to slop out their cells. Ordinary prisoners would have had to do that duty for them and it was a very gruesome task. IRA prisoners would have been the biggest grouping in Portlaoise and they probably would have been the top dogs in the prison at the time. The Provisional IRA prisoners operated a command structure where they had a senior officer in command and when an IRA prisoner had a request for the governor, it was his commanding officer who went in to talk and make the request on behalf of that detainee.

A Fine Gael/Labour government was in coalition and they were determined to break the command structure of the Provos and, as a result, more stringent searches were introduced in the prison. Obviously, because the IRA had a very structured command within the jail themselves, they were eager to smuggle in to the prison anything they could—explosives, weapons, bullets—and this was something the government wanted to stop. That is the main reason why tensions in the prison were so high at the time. 'I remember wondering at the time, and again in the immediate aftermath of the shooting,' says Kieran, 'if there could have been any way that our dad may have been a hard ass, so to speak, to some individual prisoner or grouping in the prison at the time. But we knew him well enough to realise that he just wasn't like that and could never be like that, to anyone. He had expressed to us so many times down through the years that even though these fellows were incarcerated, they were still human beings, they deserved to see out their time and they deserved to be shown some respect. There was no way that he would have been physically violent or physically brutal to any individual prisoner.

'I can certainly see how it would be in the interest of other groups or other individuals out there to put that spin on the story, but quite frankly those paramilitary groups back through the years have made statements in terms of their involvement in various cases and their motives behind them, and they have subsequently been proved to be lying. Our dad never laid a hand on us as kids and we know he didn't have it in him to be evil to anyone. And none of his colleagues have ever even hinted to us that he was aggressive in work.'

Kieran admits that they may never find out the full story behind what happened the night his father was shot, and why the hit was ordered. But he says they will keep fighting for the truth. 'Every time I think back on the life my dad was left with after that attack, it makes me even more determined to find the truth. He was taken from us in a very cowardly way. I mean he was just walking out of a boxing match when he heard footsteps coming from behind him and before he could look around an assailant gets off a motorbike, walks up from behind and shoots him in the back of the neck. Not only was it horrific for him but it was terrible for everybody else there who saw it happen, all of his friends who had to watch him being shot down in cold blood.

'He was a man in the prime of his life,' says Kieran, 'very healthy, a fit man with three young kids and a young wife and suddenly he couldn't do anything for himself. My mam and my aunt, who is a nurse, cared for him all the time. But his life was reduced to sitting in a rotary bed for 12 or 15 hours a day and then having to be lifted with a hoist, which we had installed into the family home, and put into a wheelchair. It was very sad for us all as a family to have to go through that.'

After the shooting, it was nearly two months before Sheila brought her sons to the Rehabilitation Hospital to see their father. They knew she was trying to protect them and it was hard for the three boys to see their dad lying on a rotary bed in an isolated room with a lot of medical equipment attached to him, just to keep him alive. At the time, Brian was still on a respirator and wasn't able to breathe on his own. 'He was still in a coma and I remember thinking, How could it have happened to us,' says Kieran. 'It was hard to accept at our age that he couldn't talk to us. He was just lying there. You might just get a flicker of his eyelids every now or then but that was it. It was very upsetting.

'We didn't have a normal life at all back then because mam was in the hospital with dad all the time and everything was so different. We were used to doing things at the weekends with dad and suddenly there was nothing. And when he came home it was just as bad because mam had to be there day and night for him. And he was just a different person. We had hoped that when he came out of the coma, he would be back to being our 'dad' but we were too young to understand really. It was heartbreaking to see him not being able to play football or mess around with us like he used to do. The man who shot our dad took everything away from us that night. He destroyed all of our lives, not just our dad's.'

Austin doubts the family will ever get all the details in relation to his father's case.

'As a family, we have been looking for justice for quite some time now, and for us as a unit, it does take a lot out of us. A lot of my spare time and Kieran's and Oliver's has gone into trying to dig up different information, going to meet guys who may have known something about what happened. Some months, my mobile phone bills go through the roof because I could be on one call for half an hour hoping that the information coming from the other end might just be something that would finally make someone sit up and take notice. A lot of people have said to me over the years, "Look, Austin, what is it that you hope to get out of all this in the end?" And what I'm hoping is at the end of this for us, as a family, is justice.

'I have no great desire to see somebody locked up, caged, and the key thrown away. What I do have a desire to see is somebody stand before their peers in a court of law and to be convicted and found guilty of this atrocity. It was an assassination of a senior servant of the state. The state, to my mind, and those of my brothers and my mother, has not stepped up to the mark to help us out in any way with regard to this. There is no fitting memorial anywhere within the prison service to my father. The Minister for Justice gave us an undertaking when we met him that this would be looked at and still nothing has been done.'

Many people have told Austin that he isn't going to get any-where with his questions, that the state will grind him down and he won't get the justice he wants. But he also knows that if some-body is convicted in court, then the Good Friday Agreement comes into play. 'The Good Friday Agreement is not something that I'm happy about in that there are people who committed heinous atrocities out there roaming the streets now because of it, but I have got my head around it and I think the rest of the family has and we realise that if someone is convicted of this they're probably not going to do any serious jail time for it. But what we do want for closure is somebody to be charged and sentenced and for that conviction to be registered against somebody's name and that they are on licence for the rest of their lives.

'When it comes to closure I'm afraid we may never, as a family, get the outcome we want. If somebody is convicted for the assassination of my father and the work colleague who I believe set him up is charged, then we will finally get some peace, but I firmly believe that my father died because of something within the prison, something to do with a colleague and what my father had been investigating and I don't think that will ever come out. I don't think we will ever get to the bottom of that one. That's a shame because my father worked as an upstanding servant of the state and in his job he strived, to the best of his ability, to make sure that the state was protected at all times. He was liked by both prisoners and colleagues and yet no one has given him the recognition he deserves by getting to the bottom of why he was killed. And that is very sad.'

The other concern Austin has is that young people joining the prison service today are not being made aware of what happened to his father, and are not being made aware of the dangers of being a prison officer. He doesn't think many of them would even know what happened to his father and this is something that he thinks should be addressed. He would like some sort of recognition from within the service of the work his father was doing. He feels that people need to know that the reason his father was killed was directly related to his job and that it was directly related to the fact that his father was doing his job so well.

'The state has basically abdicated their responsibility to my father and to what he was trying to do in Portlaoise at the time. Luckily, I've never felt uncomfortable working in the prison service knowing what I know—that another member of the service could have set my father up to be assassinated. I'm a fairly thick-skinned individual and things like that don't really worry me. I'm the type of a person who goes into work on a day to day basis and I do my job and I do what I have to do without thinking about things like that. If I was to think about it, I would never have gone into the prison service at all, or if I thought that it was affecting my work, I would have left it a long time ago.'

Austin enjoys his job and enjoys the camaraderie of his colleagues. 'I have good friends within the prison and I can see a positive end to what the modern prison service is trying to do in relation to areas like rehabilitation. But I have to say that I think that the state has been very complacent in relation to what happened to my dad and I know that probably doesn't sit too easily with maybe some senior civil servants in the Irish prison service. But, as a prison officer in a management grade, I have never had a problem going in to work, doing my job as I'm supposed to do it and coming home every evening feeling that maybe I have achieved something. I have to get on with things every day, just as my own father did.'

Sheila Stack is still very angry that 25 years later nothing has changed in relation to her husband's case. To this day, it is regarded by the gardaí as an open murder case and is listed on the files of the Cold Case Unit but no one knows if, or when, it will ever be solved.

'It's a very hard thing for us all to deal with because Brian worked for the state and the state, in my opinion, has really let him down by not bringing the perpetrators to justice. The hurt is still there, it's always there. But you just have to deal with it. Different days brings different feelings, but you have to deal with them as best you can. Some days are easier than others. But what we need now is justice. To see someone charged with Brian's murder. He worked all his life for the state and I think the state owes him that, to give him some form of justice.

'In my opinion, Brian was murdered because he was too good at his job, he was too eager to do the best job possible for the state and now it's time for the state to acknowledge that.'